Making Sense of Latin Documents for Family & Local Historians

Brooke Westcott

THE FAMILY HISTORY PARTNERSHIP

Published by
The Family History Partnership
57 Bury New Road, Ramsbottom
Bury, Lancashire BL0 0BZ

www.thefamilyhistorypartnership.com

First published 2014

Copyright © Brooke Westcott

ISBN: 978 1 906280 45 1

Printed and bound by
Berforts Information Press
Southfield Road, Eynsham
Oxford OX29 4JB

CONTENTS

Introduction and Parish Registers	3
Wills	8
Probates	14
Inventories	24
Intestacy	26
Citations	31
Interrogatories	33
Definitive Sentence or Final Decree	36
Excommunication	45
Writs	49
Inquisitions Post Mortem	54
Land Deeds	61
Final Concord	71
Recovery of Seisin	75
Copyholds and Surrenders	80

INTRODUCTION AND PARISH REGISTERS

The farther back your researches take you, the more likely you are to come across documents partially or wholly in Latin. Index entries and catalogue descriptions vary in completeness, and it can be dispiriting sometimes to find that a document contains no more information than its catalogue entry. But if you don't go through it word for word you will always wonder whether something vital was hidden in there somewhere.

The aim of this book is to act as a crib; to set out and translate the basic form of the most useful and most common Latin documents, enabling the genealogist to get the most out of them. It is not a guide to reading old handwriting or translating Latin, although, unfortunately, you need to be reasonably competent in both of these to understand Latin documents.

It is difficult to teach yourself Latin, and the number of people who have had any grounding at school is dwindling by the year. At the time of writing the Open University offers a course in classical Latin, and some other universities run summer schools.

Learning to read old handwriting is a slightly simpler matter. If you work on English documents of the eighteenth century and earlier you will come across the same contraction marks as in Latin writing. The letter p, for example, can be written with additional strokes, loops and curls to denote per-, par-, pre- and pro-. There are various books, websites and courses available to help with palaeography.

The words of the original document may be heavily abbreviated (letters cut off the end) or contracted (letters missed from the middle) but I have expanded them. I could say "silently" expanded them, as I have not followed the convention of using square brackets to indicate the omitted letters. However it should not be difficult to match the shortened versions with the full ones.

I have given the translations one sentence or part-sentence at a time because the standard phrases do not always occur in the expected order. It should then be possible for the translator to see exactly where certain phrases have come from and how they contribute to the final translation.

Readers familiar with classical Latin will soon notice differences between that and medieval Latin.
(1) The English word order is often followed, rather than leaving verbs to the end of the sentence.
(2) The letter combination *ae* is often replaced by *e*. As a result, if you need to find the meaning of a word beginning with *pre-*, you may have to look in your dictionary under *prae-*, and so on.
(3) The letter *t* is often replaced by *c*.

(4) The verbs *sum* and *eram*, used to construct the perfect and pluperfect passive in classical Latin, are replaced by *fui* and *fueram* in medieval Latin. So "the burden of execution was granted to Jane Smith" comes out as *onus execucionis commissum fuit Jane Smith* rather than *onus executionis Janae Smith commissum est*;

(5) The distinction between *sui* and *eius* is blurred if not entirely lost. In classical Latin, "Peter saw John and his wife" would be *Petrus Johannem et uxorem suam vidit* if the woman was Peter's wife, and *Petrus Johannem et uxorem eius vidit* if the woman was John's wife. Medieval scribes tended to think the word "his" and write the word *eius* without stopping to consider syntax, so you can only work from the context.

Parish register entries demonstrate some of these peculiarities but have the advantage of being short and predictable. They also give you a chance to brush up on gender- and case- endings; *filia*, feminine, daughter; *filius*, masculine, son. But don't fall into the trap of thinking that a word ending in *-a* must be feminine. Remember *nauta* (sailor) and *agricola* (farmer). The Latin for Thomas is *Thoma*, and "of Thomas" is *Thomae* or *Thome*.

Baptism:
Baptizationes infantium
Baptisms of infants
De baptisatis mense Novembris Anno predicto
Concerning those baptised in the month of November in the year aforesaid
Vicesimo septimo die Emma filia Johannis Smith et Anne uxoris eius baptizata fuit
On the 27th day Emma the daughter of John Smith and Ann his wife was baptized

Why "Ann", not "Anne", in the last translation? Because however her name was spelt in English, the vicar or priest translated it as *Anna*, and then changed the last letter to *e* to indicate the genitive (possessive) case. It is impossible to work backwards and arrive at the original spelling, so it is good practice to choose the simpler. Probability might help. Someone described as *Jacobus* in Latin was almost certainly James, not Jacob, in English.

Burial:
Sepulturae Anno Predicto
Burials in the year aforesaid
De sepultis mense Novembris Anno predicto
Concerning those buried in the month of November in the year aforesaid
Sara Taylor vidua sepulta fuit
Sarah Taylor, widow, was buried

Marriage entries come in a larger variety as there were several ways to denote marriage:

Nuptie Anno Predicto
Marriages in the year aforesaid

Matrimonium solemnizatum fuit inter Johannem Smith et Elizabetham Jones
A marriage was solemnized between John Smith and Elizabeth Jones. [Their names are in the accusative case because *inter* governs the accusative.]

Johannes Smith duxit in matrimonio Elizabetham Jones
John Smith led Elizabeth Jones into matrimony. [Nominative case for him, being the subject of the sentence; accusative for her, being the object.]

Elizabeth Jones nupta fuit Johanni Smith
Elizabeth Jones was married to John Smith. [Nominative case for her, being the subject of the sentence; dative for him, to indicate "to". *nupta* feminine, to agree Elizabeth.]

Johannes Smith et Elizabeth Jones nupti fuere
John Smith and Elizabeth Jones were married. [*nupti* masculine plural, to include both groom and bride. *fuere* a rare alternative to *fuerunt*; see paragraph below about erudite clerks.]

Johannes Smith et Elizabeth Jones in matrimonio coniuncti sunt
John Smith and Elizabeth Jones were joined in matrimony

Why sunt, not fuerunt, in the last example? I indicated above that "were joined" would be written as *coniuncti fuerunt* in medieval Latin, but Parish Registers were only introduced in 1538, which is hardly medieval. In the renaissance there was a movement back towards classical Latin, so you may well find the priest liked to flaunt his education, and took care to write *coniuncti sunt* when he meant "were joined".

Miscellaneous:

Natus/nata fuit	He/she was born
Eodem die	On the same day
Ultimo die	On the last day
Penultimo die	On the second-last day
Ibidem	In the same place
Coelebs	Bachelor/spinster
Vidua/viduus	Widow/widower
Rector huius ecclesie	Rector of this church
Sponsor	Godparent

The use of Latin in public records was prohibited in 1733, but it was not compulsory before then, and many early Church of England registers are in English. Likewise Roman Catholic registers; these were the priest's private records, and the choice of language was his.

Normally a marriage would require the calling of banns, but this could be avoided by obtaining a marriage licence. The procedure involved one of the parties entering into a bond and undertaking to pay a penalty if any impediment to the marriage came to light. The opening section of such Marriage Bonds or Allegations was in Latin but followed the same format as that in the example of an Administration Bond given at the end of the chapter on intestacy.

Don't forget that before 1752 the number of the year changed on 25th March, not 1st January. So for example 31st December 1650 was followed by 1st January 1650, then some three months later came 24th March 1650, followed by 25th March 1651. This is the system in use when a date is given "according to the computation and reckoning of the Church of England."

Occasionally, particularly on monumental inscriptions, the Roman system of Kalends and Nones is used. If you are lucky you may find a table of such dates somewhere in your dictionary. The Collins Gem Latin Dictionary also has a table for numerals, and even a family tree showing the Latin terms for various relationships. As well as a dictionary, you may find it useful to have some or all of the following;

Gooder, Eileen A. Latin for Local History: An Introduction. Longman. ISBN-13 978-0582487284
Kennedy's Revised Latin Primer. Longman. ISBN-13 978-0582362406
Latham, R.E. Revised Medieval Latin Word-List. Oxford University Press. ISBN-13 978-0197258910
Marshall, Hilary. Palaeography for Family and Local Historians. Phillimore & Co Ltd. ISBN-13 978-1860776519
Morris, Janet. A Latin Glossary for Family and Local Historians. The Family History Partnership. ISBN-13 978-1906280185
Sidwell, Keith. Reading Medieval Latin. Cambridge University Press ISBN-13 978-0521447478
Stuart, Denis. Latin for Local & Family Historians. The History Press. ISBN-13 978-1860773853
Thorley, John. Documents in Medieval Latin. Gerald Duckworth & Co Ltd. ISBN-13 978-0715628171
Martin, Charles Trice. The Record Interpreter. Phillimore & Co Ltd. ISBN-13 978-0850334654
Cheney, C.R. Jones, Michael (Editor). A Handbook of Dates. Cambridge University Press. ISBN-13 978-0521778459

Websites giving help with palaeography and documents in Latin include;
University of Nottingham – Manuscripts and Special Collections – Research Guidance – Deeds in Depth
The National Archives – Online Palaeography Tutorial

WILLS

After someone dies their possessions have to be disposed of. In the past, as today, only a small proportion of the population made wills. Usually a person's few belongings passed down the family without dispute, often before the owner's death.

Some people, of a tidy mind, choose to make a will even if it is not really necessary. A spinster's will may contain many small bequests to relatives and friends. Others are compelled to make a will, because they are wealthy, or their affairs complicated, or they anticipate a dispute if they leave the family to sort matters out between themselves.

Whatever the situation, someone will have to obtain legal authority to take control of the assets, convert them into cash if necessary, pay debts and legacies if any, and dispose of the balance.

This person is known in general terms as the Personal Representative. If there is a will, the personal representative will usually be the Executor (masculine) or Executrix (feminine) appointed therein. His or her legal authority will consist of a Grant of Probate. If there is no will, or no executor or executrix is named, the personal representative will be somebody with an interest in the matter, such as the next of kin or a creditor, and the legal authority will consist of the issue of Letters of Administration, often shortened to Admon.

In the past a will might only have been made when serious illness struck, or the writer was about to undertake a long journey or other risky enterprise. The testator wrote his will, usually in English, or at least decided who was to get what. If there was time he might then call in professional assistance – a lawyer to consider the full legal position, or a scrivener, or the local vicar – to make sure he hadn't forgotten anything obvious like naming an executor or a guardian for his children, and then to write out the will in standard form, possibly in Latin. If time was short, a nuncupative will, ie a deathbed statement before witnesses, might be the only option.

Medieval wills reflect the preoccupations of the times. Wealth poured into the great churches and cathedrals. Charities were established and colleges endowed, all in the hope of recognition in the life everlasting.

A fitting send-off was considered essential. Wax was provided by the pound for burning on the day of the funeral, or in the form of "torches", large candles for the altar. Priests, canons and chaplains were promised so much per head to attend the funeral service, perform the obsequies, pray for the deceased's soul, and celebrate masses in remembrance. A common request was for a trental, a series of thirty masses. The octave, a service a week after the funeral, and the month's mind, one month after, had to be provided for, as did a service on the anniversary, and possibly others in later years. Some priests took the money without performing the duties, hence the common stipulation that an "honest priest of good fame" be found.

Bequests were made for church repairs and improvements; to the fabric, the windows, the bells, the seating. A sense of community is also apparent from sums left for building roads, repairing bridges, providing dowries for poor girls or freeing debtors from prison. A good turnout at the funeral could be encouraged by providing gowns for paupers, conditional on attendance.

Gifts to family and servants often took the form of a cow or a sheep, or a bushel of wheat, corn or barley. Gilded goblets and furred and lined gowns give a vivid impression of the lifestyle of the moneyed classes of the middle ages.

Almost without exception a will begins with the phrase, *In dei nomine amen*, or its English translation, "In the name of God Amen."

The date usually follows, sometimes in terms of the year of the monarch's reign, alternatively (or additionally) in the modern *Anno Domini* form. Where both are given the phrase *Annoque Domini,* meaning "*and* in the year of Our Lord" may be used.

> *In dei nomine amen*
> In the name of God, Amen.
> *… die mensis … Anno Domini Millesimo CCCC ^{mo} xlviij ^{vo}*
> on the … day of the month of … in the year of our Lord 1448 [literally "one thousand 400th 48th"]
> *Ego … vidua compos mentis et bone/sane memorie existens*
> I, …, widow, being whole of mind and of good/healthy memory
> *licet eger corporis / eger tamen corpore*
> albeit weak of body /weak, however, in body
> *condo testamentum meum in hunc modum*
> make my testament in this manner.

Next comes the committal; a section commending the deceased's soul into God's care, and making arrangements for the burial of his body. Often the testator asks to be buried in his local parish church. The precise form of the committal varies but it was usually taken from a book of standard legal precedents. The resulting religious tone may not necessarily indicate the testator's own beliefs. More reliable guides to your ancestor's philosophy may be found in the manner in which he wishes his children to be brought up, in his choice of reading matter ("my book of the lives of the saints"), or in the inscriptions he suggests for personalised mementoes. Even these may be a matter of convention rather than choice though.

> *Inprimis/Imprimis commendo/do/lego animam meam deo omnipotenti beate Marie virgini matri sue et omnibus sanctis*
> First I commend/give/leave my soul to almighty God, to the blessed virgin Mary his mother, and to all the saints,
> *corpusque meum ad sepeliendum*
> and my body to be buried
> *in cimiterio ecclesie parochialis de …*
> in the churchyard of the parish church of …
> *in sancta sepultura ubicumque contingerit me mori*
> in holy burial wherever I may happen [literally "it may happen me"] to die

Certain bequests were compulsory, or effectively so by force of custom and practice,

> *Item lego optimam bestiam meam nomine mortuarii mei secundum consuetudinem patrie*
> Item I leave my best beast in the name of my mortuary [customary gift claimed by the incumbent from the estate of a deceased parishioner] according to the custom of the country
> *Item pro decimis meis oblitis et negligenter solutis xij d*
> Item for my tithes forgotten and negligently paid 12d
> *Item lego summo altari eiusdem ecclesie xij d*
> Item I leave to the high altar of the same church 12d
> *Item ad reparacionem dicte ecclesie …*
> Item to the repair of the said church …
> *Item fabrice predicte ecclesie …*
> Item to the fabric of the aforesaid church …
> *Item lego matrici ecclesie nostre …*
> Item I leave to our mother church of …
> *Item lego iiij libras cere incendi circa corporem meum in die sepulture mee*
> Item I leave 4 pounds of wax to be burned around my body on the day of my burial.
> *Item lego cuilibet sacerdoti existenti ad obsequia mea viij d*
> Item I leave to each priest being present at my funeral service 8d.
> *Item immediate ad celebrandum pro anima mea et animabus omnium fidelium defunctorum unum trentale/trigintale missarum x s*
> Item to celebrate one trental of masses [series of thirty masses] immediately, for my soul and the souls of all the deceased faithful, 10s
> *Item in die trentale/trigintale ad celebrandum in ecclesia de … predicta et dare pauperibus iiij*^{or} *marcas*
> Item to celebrate ["mass" understood] on the day of my month's mind in the church of … aforesaid, and to give to paupers, 4 marks

There may be a series of specific gifts or bequests. Anyone standing to gain under the terms of a will is known as a beneficiary. After making all his specific legacies the testator will nominate a person or persons to receive or share the rest of his estate. This remainder is known as the residue, and those who receive it as the residuary beneficiaries. This can explain why so many specific bequests consist of "second rate" articles; "my lesser brass cauldron", "my small standing basin" etc. If a testator wanted his wife to have the best of the household goods, he might find it more convenient to make her the residuary beneficiary and leave his sons and daughters only the second best.

> *Residuum vero omnium bonorum et catallorum meorum non legatorum neque donatorum*
> The residue, indeed, of all my goods and chattels not bequeathed or given
> *debitis et legatis meis solutis*
> my debts and legacies having been paid [ablative absolute]

> *do et lego ... filio meo quem condo/facio et ordino executorem meum*
> I give and leave to ... my son, whom I make and ordain my executor
> *ad persolvendum et implendum debita ac legata mea*
> to pay and perform my debts and legacies
> *ut disponat pro salute anime mee et pro animabus omnium parentum et benefactorum meorum*
> in order that he might dispose [of my goods] for the health of my soul and for the souls of all my ancestors and benefactors [*parentum* has a wider sense than the modern "parent" and could also mean "kinsmen"]
> *prout ei melius videbitur deo placere et animam meam prodesse*
> just as may seem best to him to please God [*deo* not *deum* because *placere* takes the dative] and to benefit my soul

It was not unusual to nominate a child as executor, and not unknown for the child to be unborn. This seems to have been a safeguard to ensure the eventual inheritance was protected. In these cases however the church would appoint an adult to act as executor "during the minority of age of the executor named in the will." There could be several successive grants if the nominees died while the child was still under age.

As well as nominating an executor, the testator would often appoint one or more trusted relatives, friends or neighbours, as overseers or supervisors. They were expected to see that the terms of the will were carried out, and to offer support and advice to the executor or executrix.

> *Supervisorem presentis testamenti mei constituo ...*
> I constitute ... overseer of my present testament ...
> *Huius autem testamenti mei fideliter exequendum hos constituo executores meos videlicet ... et ...*
> Moreover I constitute these people as my executors of this my will, faithfully to execute it, that is to say, ... and ...

Finally he signed the will in front of witnesses, who also signed at the same time. Nowadays, to reduce the incidence of fraud, a witness cannot also be a beneficiary, but this provision was only introduced in 1837.

> *In cuius rei testimonium huic testamento meo sigillum meum apposui*
> In witness whereof to this my will I have affixed my seal
> *Datum die et anno supradictis*
> Given on the day and year abovesaid

Strictly, a will deals with real estate, ie freehold or copyhold land. A testament deals with personalty, ie cash, debts, leasehold land, chattels, livestock, stock-in-trade, etc. Again strictly, a gift of land is called a devise, and a gift of personal property a bequest. The common phrase, "give, devise and bequeath," is not precise, but covers all possibilities.

Although I have suggested that something in the format above would be a will, these clauses deal only with personalty, and therefore strictly constitute a testament. The testament was therefore often followed by a last will, dealing with realty, ie land.

> *Ultima voluntas eiusdem*
> The last will of the same
> *Hec est ultima voluntas mei ...*
> This is the last will of me, ...
> *facta et per me declarata die et anno supradictis*
> made and declared by me on the day and year abovesaid.
> *In primis feoffati mei scilicet ... et ... post decessum meum vendant quatuor acras terre iacentes in parochia de ...*
> First my feoffees, that is to say, ... and ..., should, after my decease, sell four acres of land lying in the parish of ...

The will is often in English even if the testament is in Latin. The distinction between the two was blurred in 1540, when the Statute of Wills allowed them to be combined in one document called the last will and testament. The use of Latin for wills died out fairly quickly thereafter.

Often the testator instructed that successive beneficiaries were to receive their portions in successive years after his decease. This enabled them to be spread over a number of harvests or breeding seasons, in an age when wealth tended to be measured in terms of crops and livestock. The testator will often dispose of freehold property outright, or if leasehold, will leave his wife or son the years remaining under the lease. Sometimes, though, he stipulates that after his death his property is to pass to his wife or son or the longer living of them. This reflects the "three lives" tenancy by which copyhold land was commonly held. Similarly he may leave the property to someone on condition that they pay the appropriate heriot.

These circumstances indicate that the transaction would also have appeared in Manorial Records. If these have survived, and can be located, they will be well worth searching. Using these records can enable land to be tracked from father to son for several generations, even where other wills or parish registers are not available.

Sometimes a man left his wife or mother the occupation and use of a property during her lifetime, after which it was to descend to his son. He may stipulate that it should do so *sine impeticione vasti* – without impeachment of waste. Impeachment of Waste was a legal action claiming damages for deterioration of the property.

The land may be put in the hands of trustees or feoffees, who hold the land in their names while making it available to a specified class of beneficiaries. These provisions, known as trusts or entails, serve a number of purposes, such as keeping the land in the family, or protecting it from wastrels or tax collectors. Procedures for creating and defeating trusts have occupied the best legal minds for centuries.

> *Inprimis volo quod ... uxor mea habeat post decessum meum omnia terras et tenementa mea ad terminum vite sue*
> First I will that ... my wife should have, after my decease, all my land and tenements, for the term of her life
> *Et post decessum predicte ... predicta terre et tenementa remaneant ... filio meo sibi et heredibus de corpore suo legitime procreatis*
> And after the decease of the aforesaid ... the aforesaid lands and tenements should remain to ... my son, to him and the heirs of his body lawfully begotten
> *Et si predictus ... obierit sine herede de corpore suo legitime procreato tunc volo quod predicta terre et tenementa remaneant fratribus suis viventibus illis heredibus et assignatis eorum imperpetuum*
> And if the aforesaid ... should die without an heir of his body lawfully begotten, then I will that the aforesaid lands and tenements should remain to his brothers [then] living, to them, their heirs and assigns for ever

Where there was time for a "fair copy" its writer might act as one of the witnesses, adding the Latin word *scriptor* (writer) after his signature, or putting the phrase *per me* (by me) before it.

At one time the will was copied into an Act Book and the original returned to the family. This arrangement was of course susceptible to fraud. The will could be rewritten, and if the alteration ever came to light the fraudster would accuse the church of having copied it incorrectly.

The procedure was therefore changed so that the church kept the original and a copy was given to the family. A copy might already have been prepared by the family and would just need checking. If not, a full transcript was prepared and charged to the deceased's estate. The family's copy of the will might be handed over as the legal title for the next owner of the deceased's residence or other lands, and therefore be preserved with that family's muniments or estate papers.

In many places the register copy was still made even though the original had been retained. The word *Examinatur* (it is examined), abbreviated to *Ex*, may appear at the end of the register entry, to show that the copy has been compared with the original.

Sometimes the note *iur'*, short for *iuratus* (sworn), is inserted by or above the names of the appropriate people in the register copy of the will, to show that they have made the required oath.

Duplicate copies, duly authorised and bearing the official grant, known as probate copies, were also supplied if required.

PROBATES

If someone made a will it was taken after their death to the appropriate probate court to be proved, that is, accepted as valid. Exactly which was the appropriate court before 1858 depended on the location of the deceased's personalty. There are a number of books explaining which wills can be found where, and how to go about a search.

Whichever court was involved it would almost certainly have been an ecclesiastical court, that is, one controlled by the church. These courts had no jurisdiction over gifts of freehold property. If such devises were in dispute they had to be settled at Chancery or Common Law. Nonetheless the will was still registered in the ecclesiastical court if it mentioned any personalty at all.

The executors swore a standard oath, to administer the estate faithfully and in accordance with the terms of the will, and were given legal authority to dispose of it. This was the Grant of Probate. It was written on or attached to the will and a copy was kept with the court's records.

Although most grants of probate convey the same information, each registry tended to have its own form of words, which got longer as the centuries passed. A typical medieval probate would be as follows.

> *Probatum fuit apud ... coram magistro ... ... die mensis ... anno domini ... et commissa est/fuit administratio executoribus in eodem testamento nominatis*
> [This will] was proved at ... before Master ... on the ... day of the month of ... in the year of our Lord ... and administration is/was granted to the executors named in the same will.

The relevant court would probably have been an Archdeacon's court; possibly a Bishop's, or Consistory, court; maybe one administered by a Bishop's deputy, or Commissary court; or perhaps an Archbishop's, or Prerogative court. Some areas had "peculiar jurisdiction", meaning that they were independent some or all of the time. The following phrases are likely to feature in their probates.

> *Decanus de ... certificavit de approbatione huiusmodi testamenti per omnes testes in eodem testamento nominatos*
> The Dean of ... certified approval of this will [*testamentum* can safely be translated as "will" unless an *ultima voluntas* "last will" is also mentioned] by all the witnesses named in the same will
> *Probatum approbatum et insinuatum fuit/erat hoc/huiusmodi/presens testamentum retroscriptum / suprascriptum ... nuper parochie ... in comitatu ... defuncti*
> This present/before-written / above-written will of ... late of the parish of ... in the county of ..., deceased, was proved, approved and favoured
> *unacum ultima voluntate eiusdem*
> together with the last will of the same

apud ..., ... die mensis ... anno domini ...
at ..., on the ... day of the month of ... in the year of our Lord ...
coram venerabili viro Magistro ... legum Doctore
before the worshipful [*viro*, "man", can be ignored] Master ... Doctor of Laws
Officiali Principali / Commissario
Official Principal / Commissary
Reverendi in Χριστο patris ac domini domini ... providencia/permissione divina Episcopi ... vicario generali
Vicar General of the Reverend Father and Lord in Christ, ..., by divine providence/permission Lord Bishop of ...,
legitime deputato
lawfully deputed
per ... filium naturalem et legitimum retronominati defuncti et executorem unicum in hoc testamento nominatum
by ... the natural and lawful son of the beforenamed deceased, and the sole executor named in this will
juramentis testium supranominatorum
by the oaths of the witnesses abovenamed
ac approbatum etc
and approved etc
commissumque fuit/est onus execucionis dicti testamenti
and the burden of execution of the said will was/is committed,
necnon commissa fuit et est administratio omnium et singulorum bonorum catallorum creditorum et iurium dicti defuncti
and indeed administration of all and singular the goods, chattels, credits and rights of the said deceased
infra Archidiaconatum ... pertinentium ad eum vite et mortis sui tempore
belonging to him within the Archdeaconry of ... in his lifetime [literally "at the time of life"] and at the time of his death
et omnium qualitercumque concernentium dictum testamentum
and of all matters of any sort whatsoever concerning the said will, was and is committed,
... vidue relicte dicti defuncti et executrici in dicto testamento nominate
to ..., widow, the relict of the said deceased and the executrix named in the said will
primitus/prius in debita iuris forma iurato/iurate de bene etc
he/she having been first sworn in due form of law well etc [to administer the same]
salvo iure cuiuscumque
saving all rights whatsoever [literally, "saving the right of any person whomsoever"].

Sometimes one court usurped another's authority, perhaps because of an Ecclesiastical Visitation, or because the usual court had no authority at that particular time. This might happen, for example, after the death of a Bishop and before the appointment of his successor. In this case there was a period of *sede vacante*; literally, "the seat being vacant".

Towards the end of the 18th Century it became more and more common to prove wills at the Prerogative Court of Canterbury. This court had previously only been used for the estates of wealthy people and those dying overseas. By the time centralised arrangements were introduced in 1858 most English and Welsh wills

Probate of a Will proved at the Prerogative Court of Canterbury. From The National Archives, reference PROB11/24. Will of Henry Lodington, Citizen and Grocer of London, proved 13 December 1531. The initial letters of Testamentum and Lamhith (Lambeth) have been adapted into cartoon characters.

were already being proved in London, due in no small part to a Bank of England ruling in 1810 that it would only recognise grants of probate from the PCC.

And so, next, the one which eventually superseded all the others; a grant from the Prerogative Court of Canterbury (PCC);

> *Probatum fuit huiusmodi testamentum suprascriptum apud London*
> This above-written will was proved at London
> *unacum codicillo eidem annexo*
> together with a codicil annexed to the same
> *coram magistro / venerabili viro ... legum doctore / artium magistro / sacre theologie professore*
> before Master / the worshipful ... Doctor of Laws / Master of Arts / Professor of Sacred Theology
> *Surrogato venerabilis et egregii viri/domini ... militis legum etiam doctoris Curie Prerogative Cantuariensis Magistri Custodis sive Commissarii legitime constituto*
> Surrogate, lawfully constituted, of the worshipful and distinguished man/Sir ... , knight, also Doctor of Laws, Master, Keeper or Commissary of the Prerogative Court of Canterbury
> *... die mensis ... anno domini ...*
> on the ... day of the month of ... in the year of our Lord ...
> *juramento/juramentis executoris/executorum in testamento nominati/nominatorum*
> by the oath/s of the executor/s named in the will
> *in persona ... procuratoris sui in hac parte*
> in the person of ... his proctor in this regard
> *Ac approbatum et insinuatum*
> And approved and favoured
> *Cui/quibus commissa fuit administracio omnium et singulorum bonorum jurium et creditorum*
> To whom was committed administration of all and singular the goods, rights and credits
> *dicti defuncti*
> of the said deceased [or alternatively;]
> *dictum defunctum et ejus testamentum huiusmodi qualitercumque concernentium*
> in any way whatsoever concerning the said deceased and this his will [or]
> *commissaque fuit administracio etc executoribus in dicto testamento nominatis*
> and administration etc was committed to the executors named in the said will
> *ad sancta dei evangelia in debita Juris forma prius/primitus jurato/jurate/juratis*
> he/she/they having been first sworn in due form of law on God's holy gospels [This phrase actually appears towards the end of the probate but needs to be placed here to make sense of the translation]
> *de bene et fideliter administrando eadem*
> well and faithfully to administer the same
> *ac de pleno et fideli inventario omnium et singulorum bonorum et debitorum huiusmodi conficiendo citra festum ... proxime futuro exhibendo*
> and to make a full and faithful inventory of all and singular the goods and debts and to exhibit it before the feast of ... next coming [literally "in the future"]
> *necnon de plano et vero computo/compoto calculo sive ratiocinio inde etc reddendo*
> and indeed to render a plain and true account, calculation or reckoning thereof etc

salvo iure cuiuscumque
saving all rights whatsoever. [At least, this is the usual translation. But the full phrase, very rarely given, is *salvo iure cuiuscumque interesse habentis*, "saving the right of any person whomsoever having an interest".]
Examinatur
It is examined [ie register copy compared with the original]

This is a list of Masters, Keepers or Commissaries of the Prerogative Court of Canterbury. It will save struggling to decipher the names, which may then be useful for comparison purposes, especially to identify capital letters, which can be awkward. These men usually collected a knighthood for their trouble, so you may see them described as *Dominus*, Sir. (But note, the words *Dominus* and Sir don't necessarily imply a knighthood, as they were also courtesy titles for priests and academics.)

William Drury	1580's
William Lewin	1590's
John Gibson	1600's
John Bennet	1600's – 1620's
Henry Marten	1620's – 1630's
Nathaniel Brent	1640's
William Merricke	1640's – 1660's
Leoline Jenkins	1660's – 1670's
Richard Raines	1680's – 1700's
Charles Hedges	1710's
John Bettesworth	1720's – 1740's
George Lee	1750's
George Hay	1760's – 1770's
Peter Calvert	1780's
William Wynne	1780's – 1800's

If probate has been granted to only one or two of the executors rather than all of them you should see something like;

Reservata potestate
Power having been reserved
similem commissionem faciendi / consimilem administracionem committendi
of making a similar grant / of committing similar administration
... *alteri executori / ceteris coexecutoribus in huiusmodi/dicto testamento nominato/nominatis cum venerit/venerint eam petiturus/petituri*
to ..., the other executor/s named in this/the said will when he comes / they come [literally "shall have come"] seeking it
liberis dicte defuncte in minore / minori etate existentibus
to the children of the said deceased, being in minority of age [literally, "in minor age"]

cum venerint eandem in forma iuris in se suscepturis
when they shall have come to take the same upon themselves in form of law
cum ad plenam pervenerint etatem et onus etc
when they come to full age and [come seeking] the burden [of execution] etc.

A lawfully appointed executor might renounce the entitlement to act. The reason is not usually specified; the normal form of words is "for diverse reasons him/her thereunto justly moving." Sometimes it is old age or infirmity, and another family member will take over the responsibility.

Occasionally it is clear that the deceased has been living beyond his means and has died penniless. In these circumstances there is no point in anyone's taking out probate or letters of administration. They will get nothing out of it. If an executor has been appointed they are likely to refuse to act. Thus;

> *Et quia executor in huiusmodi testamento nominatus oneri execucionis eiusdem renunciavit*
> And because the executor named in this will renounced the burden of execution of the same [*oneri* because *renuncio* takes the dative]
> *ideo dominus commisit administracionem bonorum huiusmodi defuncti prefato ...*
> therefore the Lord committed administration of the goods of this deceased to the aforenamed ...

Or;

> *... et ... executoribus onus eiusdem coram nobis recusantibus ac refutantibus*
> ... and ..., the executors, refusing and refuting the burden of the same before us [ablative absolute]

Or;

> *... relicta dicti defuncti coexecutrice in eodem testamento nominata onus execucionis huiusmodi testamenti in se suscipere penitus et expresse renunciante et recusante*
> ... the relict of the said deceased, coexecutrix named in the same will, wholly and expressly renouncing and refusing to take upon herself the burden of execution of this will [ablative absolute again]

Similarly if no executor was named;

> *Et quia testator nullum executorem nominavit*
> And because the testator named no executor,
> *ideo dominus officialis commisit administracionem bonorum ...*
> therefore the Lord Official committed administration of the goods ...
> *ideo concessa fuit et est administracio bonorum dicti defuncti ...*
> therefore administration of the goods of the said deceased was and is granted
> *... et ... duobus legatariis principalibus in hoc testamento nominatis*
> to ... and ..., the two principal legatees named in this will
> *ad administrandum iuxta vim formam et effectum dicti testamenti juratis etc salvo etc*
> they having been sworn etc to administer according to the force, form and effect of the said will, saving etc.

The deceased may have left some assets, but also debts totalling a greater amount. In this case again there will be nothing left for the family and any executor will be reluctant to get involved. In this case the people who are owed money (the creditors) may get the court's permission to take over the administration of the estate. This is what has happened if you see Probate or Letters of Administration granted to the "Principal Creditor".

Sometimes there is a long delay between death and the grant of probate or letters of administration; twenty years or more. This does not mean the estate was complicated; the complexity of the estate has no bearing on the appointment of a personal representative. It usually happens where property has been disposed of within the family without any dispute. There may have been no will, or if there was one, the family may have felt no need to go to the trouble and expense of proving it. Many years later the owner of some land tries to sell it and discovers he has no legal title to do so. He then has to make good the legal position by getting a grant of representation retrospectively.

Often the executor was (or claimed to be) too old, frail or sick to travel to the court to swear an oath in person. In these circumstances a direction, known as a commission, would be sent to the executor's local vicar, telling him to administer the oath on the court's behalf. Where this has happened the following phrase occurs;

> *vigore commissionis in ea parte emanentis alibi/alias*
> by force of a commission in this regard issuing elsewhere/at another time

The commission was made by means of Letters Commissional;

> ... *Reverendi in Χριστο/Christo patris et Domini Domini ... providentia divina ... Episcopi Vicarius in spiritualibus generalis et officialis principalis legitime fulcitus*
> ... Vicar General in Spiritualities and Official Principal, lawfully founded, of the Reverend Father and Lord in Christ, ..., by divine providence, Lord Bishop of ...,
> *dilectis nobis in christo ... clerico vicario de ... diocesis ... et ... salutem et gratiam in domino*
> [sends] greeting and grace in the Lord to our beloved in Christ, ... clerk, vicar of ... in [literally "of"] the diocese of ..., and to ...
> *Cum ... infra parochiam de ... in comitatu ... et diocese predicta vidua dum vixit mentis compos et in sua sana memoria existens testamentum suum in se continens ultimam voluntatem suam rite et legitime condidit fecit et publicavit in scriptis in quo sive qua ... armigerum suum et dicti testamenti sui nominavit et constituit executorem*
> Whereas ... within the parish of ... in the county ... and in the diocese aforesaid, widow, while she lived, being whole of mind and in her healthy memory, correctly and lawfully prepared, made and published her testament in writing, containing therein her last will, in which [*quo sive qua* to cater for the fact that *testamentum* is neuter and *voluntas* is feminine] she nominated and constituted ... esquire executor of her and of her said testament,

Qui quidem executor adeo in remotis agit aliisque est impeditus negotiis ut coram nobis aut alio iudice in ea parte competenti juramentum in huiusmodi casibus prestari solitum prestitur comparere non possit

Which certain executor in fact lives in distant parts, and is hindered by other matters, so that he is not able to appear before us or another judge competent in this regard to be given the oath customarily administered [literally "customary to be administered"] in these cases,

Commissionem vobis conjunctim et divisim ex petitione partis dicti executoris ad effectum subscriptum subque modo et forma inferius descriptis concedendum et committendum fore decreverimus (iustitia id poseunte)

We have therefore decreed a commission to be granted and committed to you, jointly and severally, at the petition of the party of the said executor, to the effect underwritten, and in the manner and form within described, (justice allowing it),

Ad deferendum igitur prefato ... armigero executori testamenti sive ultime voluntatis ... vidue defuncte Juramentum in tergo presentium descriptum

To administer, therefore, to the aforenamed ... esquire, the executor of the testament or last will of ... widow, deceased, the oath described on the back of these presents,

tam de veritate testamenti presentibus annexi

both as to the veracity of the testament annexed to these presents

quam de pleno et perfecto inventario omnium et singulorum bonorum iurium et creditorum dicte defuncte exhibendi

and to exhibit a full and perfect inventory of all and singular the goods, rights and credits of the said deceased

ac de vero et fideli compoto calculo sive ratiocinio inde cum ad fuerit legitime requisitus reddendi

and to render a true and faithful account, calculation or reckoning thereof when lawfully required to do so,

necnon de bene et fideliter administrando omnia et singula bona iura credita et catalla huiusmodi defuncte

and indeed well and faithfully to administer all and singular the goods, rights, credits and chattels of the deceased,

ac de solvendo debita et legata eiusdem quatenus huiusmodi bona et cattalla ad hoc se extendunt iuxta verum eorundem valorem et iuris in ea parte exigentia

and to pay the debts and legacies of the same, so far forth as the goods and chattels will extend, according to the true worth of the same, and to the demands of the law in that regard

ceteraque omnia et singula alia faciendo excercendo expediendo et exequendo que in premissis aut circa ea necessaria fuerint seu quomodolibet opportuna

and to do, exercise, settle and execute all and singular other matters which may be necessary in the premises or thereabouts, or be in any way appropriate thereto.

vobis prefatis ... de quorum fidelitate conscientia puritate et in melius gerendis dexteritate plurimum in hac parte confidimus vices et auctoritatem nostras coniunctim et divisim committimus ac plenam in domino tenore presentium concedimus potestatem

by the tenor of these presents we commit to you the aforenamed ... jointly and severally, (in the faithfulness, knowledge and purity of whom, and in their better skill at carrying things out in this regard, we greatly confide) our standing and authority, and we grant full power in the Lord,

> *mandantes tamen et volentes quatenus huiusmodi iuramento sic dilato totum et integrum processum coram vobis coniunctim vestrumve aliquo pro se divisim habitum et factum nobis nostrove commissario aut alio judice in hac parte competente quocumque manibus vestris vel sua subscriptum aliquem fidelem nunciatum transmittatis seu transmittat ille vestrum qui has literas nostras commissionales fuerit executus unacum presentibus et testamento dicte defuncte annexo citra primum diem mensis . . . proxime future*
> ordering and willing nonetheless that (this oath having been thus carried out) you, or he of you who shall have executed [*exsequor* is a deponent verb] these our Letters Commissional, shall send to us or our Commissary, or to any other Judge whomsoever competent in this regard, some faithful announcement, subscribed with your hands or his hand, [of] all and the whole process had and done before you jointly, or before any of you for himself separately, together with these presents, and with the testament of the said deceased annexed, before the first day of the month of ... next coming.
> *Datas sub sigillo quo in hac parte utimur ... die mensis ... Anno Domini ...*
> Given under the seal which we use in this regard on the ... day of the month of ... in the year of our Lord ...

Again from Kent, the procedure surrounding the issue of the commission is set out;

> *... die mensis ... anno ... solutum pro comissione bonorum ... nuper de ... defuncti quorum emanavit commissio magistro ... vicario predicto ad onerandum ... relictam dicti defuncti de bene etc et testes super testamentum dicti defuncti et ad certificandum infra mensem*
> On the ... day of the month of ... in the year ... was paid for a commission [concerning administration] of the goods of ... late of ... deceased, [in respect] of which a commission was issued to Master ..., the vicar aforesaid, to charge ..., the relict of the said deceased, well [to administer the same] etc, and [to produce] witnesses upon the will of the said deceased, and to certify the same within a month,
> *Habet ad exhibendum inventarium citra proximam diem juridicis post festum Sancti Michaelis Archangeli proximum*
> She has to exhibit an inventory before the next law-day after the feast of Saint Michael the Archangel next.
> *... die mensis ... anno ... introducta erat commissio executa per magistrum ... vicarium de ... secundo die mensis ... et exhibitum est inventarium ad summam ...*
> On the ... day of the month of ... in the year ... the commission, executed by Master ..., Vicar of ..., on the ... day of the month of ..., was introduced, and an inventory in the sum of ... was exhibited.

Likewise the procedure surrounding renunciation of execution may be set out;

> *... die mensis ... Anno Domini ... coram magistro ...*
> On the ... day of the month of ... in the year of our Lord ..., before Master ...
> *comparuit ... Notarius Publicus unus procurator huius curie et exhibuit procuratorium suum speciale sub manu et sigillo ... fratris naturalis et legitimi cuiusdam ... nuper de ... ab intestato defuncti*

there appeared ..., Notary Public, a proctor of this court, and exhibited his special proxy under the hand and seal of ... the natural and lawful brother of a certain ..., late of ..., deceased intestate,
et nomine dicti ... oneri administracionis bonorum dicti defuncti ad omnem quemcumque iuris effectum renunciavit
and in the name of the said ..., to all effect of law whatsoever, he renounced the burden of administration of the goods of the said deceased,
petiitque dictam suam renunciacionem admitti ac administracionem bonorum defuncti predicti committi etc ... sub cautione per eum interponendo
and he sought that his said renunciation be admitted, and that administration of the goods of the aforesaid deceased be committed etc to ..., under a caution to be undertaken by him.
Unde dominus ad eius peticionem renunciacionem predictam admisit et litteras administracionis bonorum jurium et creditorum defuncti predicti dicto ... ad usum et commodum proximi consanguinei commisit
Whereupon the Lord, at his petition, admitted the aforesaid renunciation, and committed Letters of Administration of the goods, rights and credits of the aforesaid deceased to the said ... to the use and benefit of the next of kin,
primitus de bene et fideliter administrando eadem etc ad sancta etc jurato etc
he having been first sworn etc, on [God's] holy [gospels] etc, well and faithfully to administer the same etc.
Obligantur idem ... ... et ... in summa ...
The same ..., ... and ... are bound in the sum of ...
Inventarium extendit se ad summam ...
The inventory extends to the sum of ...

INVENTORIES

The ecclesiastical authorities charged a fee for the work involved in granting probates and administrations. This depended on the value of the personalty included in the estate. There was one fee for those within (*Infra*) a limit of £40, and higher rates for those above (*Supra*). In order to know which band the personalty fell into, it was necessary to value all the deceased's goods. This was done by means of an inventory.

Up to 1782 every personal representative had to produce at, or "exhibit into", the probate registry, an inventory of the deceased's goods. This involved the valuation or appraisal of his or her personal property by a number of local men (and occasionally women).

They walked round the residence, inside and out, recording and valuing everything that moved and much that didn't. They valued the deceased's livestock, known generally as "cattle" even though there may have been pigs, horses and sheep; his tangible moveable property, known as "chattels", this term being derived in turn from the word "cattle"; and some intangible property, such as leases, or debts owing to him.

Debts may be "with specialty", meaning that they were evidenced by a specific legal document such as a bond, or "without specialty". Debts might also be described as "desperate", the modern equivalent being "bad debts", ie those which are unlikely to be paid. Debts which were likely to be paid, or where there was hope of collection, were "sperate". Sometimes the word "desperate" is used to mean "large" and "sperate" to mean "small".

Freehold property did not have to be valued for the inventory, but may be mentioned where it was relevant to valuing the debts. The legal presumption was that debts were settled first out of personalty, and the real estate was only affected if there was a shortfall of personal property.

The valuations were of course in pounds, shillings and pence, halfpence and farthings, and occasionally half-farthings. The numbers themselves are often written down in roman numerals. It is hardly surprising, then, that the totals are often wrong. This is often ascribed to poor standards of numeracy. But (surprise, surprise) the majority of errors are in the estate's favour. The authorities seem to have turned a blind eye to this, as they did to the flagrant under-valuations which were often submitted. Presumably they adjusted their fee scales to compensate, and everyone went away happy.

The inventory itself would be written in English, but a note in Latin may be added acknowledging that the court has seen it;

Exhibitum fuit hoc/huiusmodi inventarium etc ... die mensis ... anno domini ...
This Inventory was exhibited on the ... day of the month of ... in the year of our Lord
iuxta computacionem ecclesie Anglicane
according to the computation of the English Church (NB not "of the Church of England"
 – that would be *ecclesie Anglie*)
per magistrum ... Notarium Publicum nomine procuratoris ... executoris / administratoris / administratricis etc
by Master ... Notary Public, in the name of proctor of ... the executor / administrator / administratrix etc,
pro vero ac pleno et integro inventario omnium et singulorum bonorum et cattallorum etc dicti defuncti
as a true and full and whole inventory of all and singular the goods and chattels etc of the said deceased
durante minore / minori etate executoris
during the minor age of the executor
sub protestacione tamen de addendo etc quod si etc
under protest however of adding etc if [further goods should come to light] etc

I must say I usually translate *sub protestacione* as if it said *cum potestate*, "with power to add ...".

The existence of an inventory may be indicated by an addition to the probate or administration clause;

Et introductum fuit inventarium in pargameno solutis iij s vj d et dictus ... et ... obligantur
And an inventory on parchment was introduced, 3s 6d having been paid, and the said ... and ... are bound [in an administration bond].
Inventarium extendit ad summam xxv^{li} vj^s x^d
The inventory extends to the sum of £25 6s 10d

INTESTACY

It may be that there was no will at all, written or oral. Death may have come quickly, or the deceased may have felt no need to make a will. He is said to have died intestate.

If he owned land or property, his descendants would need official authority to take it over. They would apply for Letters of Administration, giving the next of kin authority to distribute the estate in accordance with established rules. These could be customary or statutory, and decided who got what, depending on whether the deceased left a wife, children, brothers or sisters, and so on.

The will might have been made out in a hurry, or by someone with no legal knowledge, and omit to name an executor. Or the executor named might have died since the will was made. In such cases the court would decide who was to settle the testator's affairs, usually the next of kin. They would be granted Letters of Administration with Will Annexed, often abbreviated in record offices to "Admon with Will" or "AwW".

The standard wording for issues of Letters of Administration varies less than that for grants of probate, and typically takes the following form;

> ... die mensis ... emanavit commissio ... filio naturali et legitimo ... defuncti nuper parochie ... in comitatu ...
> On the ... day of the month of ... issued forth a commission to ... the natural and lawful son of ... deceased, late of the parish of ... in the county of ...
> ad administrandum bona iura et credita dicti defuncti de bene etc
> to administer the goods, rights and credits of the said deceased
> iurato
> he having been sworn [well etc to administer the same].

Often the date is not given as part of the entry. It is given as a heading in the register, and succeeding entries simply say, for example;

> Quo die emanaverunt littere administrationis
> On which day issued forth Letters of Administration

This version is from York;

> Dictus Magister ... certificavit se commississe administracionem bonorum ...
> The said Master ... certified himself to have committed administration of the goods of ...
> nuper de Eboraco diocesis Eboracensis abintestato (ut asseritur) defuncti
> late of York in the diocese of York, deceased, (as it is asserted), intestate,
> ... relicte dicti defuncti prius jurate (salvo etc)
> to ..., the relict of the said deceased, she having been first sworn, (saving etc).

and this from the Archdeaconry of Canterbury, Kent;

Administracio omnium et singulorum bonorum iurium et creditorum que fuerunt ... nuper de ... defuncti
Administration of all and singular the goods, rights and credits which were/belonged to ... late of ... deceased
nuper abintestati ut dicitur decedentis
lately, as it is said, dying intestate,
quorum emanavit / commissa fuit administracio
administration of which goods issued forth / was committed
... filio/relicte dicti defuncti primitus in forma iuris iurato
to ..., the son/relict of the said deceased, he having been first sworn in form of law
de fideliter administrando eadem bona tam ad solucionem debitorum et legatorum dicti defuncti quam ad usum et commoditatem prolium naturalium eiusdem defuncti
faithfully to administer the same goods, both in payment of the debts and legacies of the said deceased, and to the use and commodity of the natural children of the same deceased
et habet ad exhibendum inventarium citra primum diem mensis ... proxime solvendum v s
and he has to exhibit an inventory before the first day of the month of ... next, and to pay 5s
et dictus ... generosus et ... husbandman obligantur in viginti libris etc
and the said ... gentleman, and ... husbandman, are bound [in an administration bond] in [the sum of] twenty pounds etc
et ultimo die mensis ... extunc proxime sequentis ... generosus nuncius specialis in hac parte introduxit inventarium bonorum dicti defuncti in pergameno scriptum
and on the last day of the month of ... then next following ..., gentleman, special messenger in this regard, put in the inventory of the goods of the said deceased, written in parchment.

As with probates, the Prerogative Court of Canterbury's form of grant eventually replaced all others;

Quo die
On which day [this would have been specified in an earlier entry or page heading in the register]
emanavit commissio / commissa fuit administracio
issued forth a commission / administration was committed
... filio naturali et legitimo ... nuper de ... in parochia de ... in comitatu ...
to ..., the natural and lawful son [of] ..., late of ... in the parish of ... in the county of ...,
defuncti habentis etc
deceased [better translated as "who died"] having etc [goods sufficient to found the jurisdiction of the Prerogative Court of Canterbury]
ad administrandum bona jura et credita dicti defuncti
to administer the goods, rights and credits of the said deceased
de bene etc jurato
he having been sworn well etc [to administer]
... relicta renunciante
... the relict renouncing [ablative absolute]

Various notes may appear in the right hand margin of a PCC Administration. There are usually two dates. The first, roughly six months after the grant, is the date by which the inventory had to be exhibited. The second, roughly six months after that, is the date by which the account had to be rendered. The value of the estate and its location may also be given.

Sometimes the grant of administration rehearses all the procedure leading up to it. This example is from Derbyshire;

> *Derbie ... comparuit ... de ...*
> At Derby, on [date], there appeared ... of ...
> *et allegavit ... mortem obiisse abintestato ipsumque fuisse et esse eius fratrem naturalem et legitimum et personam etc*
> and alleged that ... died intestate, and that he was and is his natural and lawful brother, and the person etc,
> *quare petiit administracionem ejus bonorum sibi concedi*
> for which reason he sought that administration of his goods be committed to him,
> *quam Dominus sub caucione idonea et presticione juramenti soliti ei concedit*
> which the lord, under a suitable caution and the administering of the customary oath, granted to him.

And this longer one from Kent;

> *... die ... ... coram magistro ... commissario etc in edibus suis presente me ... notario publico*
> On the ... day of ..., ..., before Master ..., Commissary etc, in his rooms [or possibly his house; in classical Latin, *aedes* in the singular is a room, but in the plural it denotes a house], in the presence of me, ..., Notary Public,
> *comparuit ... qui exhibuit procuratorium suum litteratorie pro ... relicta ... nuper dum vixit de ... Cantuariensis diocesis defuncti habentis dum vixit et mortis sue tempore bona etc in diversis diocesibus Cantuariensis provincie et in diocese Cantuariense decedentis et commorantis etc*
> appeared ..., who exhibited his procuracy/proxy in writing for ..., the relict of ..., late, while he lived, of ... in the diocese of Canterbury, deceased, [who died] having, while he lived and at the time of his death, goods etc in various dioceses of the Province of Canterbury, and living and dying in the diocese of Canterbury etc,
> *et exhibuit pretensum testamentum dicti ... defuncti ac petiit ipsum approbari etc et administracionem bonorum dicti defuncti iuxta testamentum etc ... relicte in persona sui procuratoris in forma iuris committi etc*
> end exhibited the supposed will of the said ... deceased, and sought that it be approved etc, and [sought that] administration of the goods of the said deceased, according to the will etc, be committed in form of law to ..., the relict, in the person of her proctor,
> *et incontinenter ... super veritate dicti testamenti produxit quendam ... in testem super veritatem dicti testamenti quem dominus juramento oneravit etc*
> and immediately ..., concerning the veracity of the said will, produced a certain ... in witness of the veracity of the said will, whom the lord charged with an oath etc,

et quia nullus est executor nominatus ideo ad peticionem ... dominus commisit administracionem bonorum ... relicte in persona dicti procuratoris sui jurate
and because there is no executor named, the lord therefore, at the petition of ..., committed administration of the goods to ..., the relict, she having been sworn in the person of her said proctor.
Salvo jure cuiuscumque
Saving all right whatsoever.
Obligantur dicta relicta et ... de ... in ij^c libris
The said relict, and ... of ..., are bound in £200 [in an administration bond; see below.]

In an administration the church officials needed to maintain a closer control over the estate, to ensure there was no fraud or maladministration. They also needed to protect the interests of any children. For this reason they developed a system of bonds; Administration, Tuition and Curation Bonds.

The administrator of the estate, and one or two other friends or relatives, signed a legal undertaking to pay a financial penalty if certain conditions were not met. The legal undertaking itself was a Bond, and was written in Latin, following the same format as was commonly used to protect the lender of money or the grantor of a lease. In the 16th and 17th centuries the amount of the bond was roughly equal to the amount of the personalty. Later on it was sometimes double. The conditions were then listed, and these constitute the Obligation. The Bond is written first, in Latin, and the obligations follow, in English.

> *Noverint universi per presentes nos ... de ... in parochia ... in comitatu ... et ... de eadem*
> May all men, by these presents, know us, ... of ... in the parish of ... in the county of ... and ... of the same,
> *Teneri et firmiter obligari reverendo in Christo/Χριστο patri ac Domino Domino ... providentia/permissione divina Episcopo ...*
> To be held and firmly bound unto the reverend father and Lord in Christ, ..., by divine providence/permission Lord Bishop of ...
> *In ... libris bonae at legalis monetae Angliae/Magnae Britanniae solvendis eidem/dicto reverendo patri aut suo certo attornato executoribus administratoribus successoribus vel assignatis suis*
> In [the sum of] ... pounds of good and lawful money of England/Great Britain, to be paid to the same/said Reverend Father or his certain attorney, his executors, administrators, successors or assigns,
> *Ad quam quidem solucionem bene et fideliter faciendam*
> To which payment indeed, well and faithfully to be made
> *obligamus nos et quemlibet/utrumque nostrum per se pro toto et in solido*
> we oblige ourselves, and each/either of us by himself for the whole and undivided [amount]
> *heredes executores et administratores nostros et cuiuslibet nostrum firmiter per presentes*
> [and we oblige] our heirs, executors and administrators, and those of each of us, firmly by these presents
> *sigillis nostris sigillatum*
> sealed with our seals

datum ... die mensis ... anno regni domini/domine nostri/nostre ... dei gratia Angliae / Magnae Britanniae Franciae et Hiberniae regis/reginae fidei defensoris etc annoque domini ...
dated the ... day of the month of ... in the ... year of the reign of our Lord/Lady ..., by the grace of God, of England/Great Britain, France and Ireland, King/Queen, defender of the faith etc, and in the year of our Lord ...

Although *datum* and *sigillatum* in the last couple of lines above do not agree with *presentes*, these are the words used on the rare occasions when *sigillat'* and *dat'* are written out in full.

In an Administration Bond the administrator would typically undertake to administer the estate fairly; to make a full inventory of the deceased's goods; to make an account of the income and outgoings during the administration period; to reappear before the Court if called upon to do so; and to hand over control to anyone who appeared with a better claim, or to anyone whom the church authorities should nominate to replace him. Helpfully, these conditions are set out in English.

In a Tuition or Curation Bond he would undertake to provide the deceased's children with accommodation, food and drink, and to educate them as appropriate to their social standing. Tuition Bonds were made out if the children were girls under 12 or boys under 14 years of age. Curation Bonds applied to children between those ages and 21.

The signing of a bond may be noted in an entry in the Act Book showing the deceased's name, the date of the bond, its value, and the names of those undertaking it. If so, the bond itself will add little information.

If you cannot read the names in the bond, look at the signatures at the bottom right of the document, which are often much easier to read. The signatures at the bottom left will be those of the church officials who prepared the bond. These often include a Notary Public, abbreviated to N.P.

Do not be fazed if you have a printed version and yet the Latin does not match exactly with the above. As the text was revised and reprinted over and over again, errors crept in; *utor* for *utro* and *obligemus* for *obligamus* at Richmond, for example.

CITATIONS

It might happen that an executor does not seek a grant of probate as quickly as he should. Perhaps he or she is quite happy living in the deceased's house and using the household goods as before. But other beneficiaries or creditors would want to get their share of the estate and might report the executor to the authorities.

Similarly, after being officially appointed, the personal representative might drag his heels and need to be called to account (literally), or to exhibit the inventory in the first place. A citation would be issued.

> ... *providentia divina Cantuariensis archiepiscopus totius Anglie primatus et metropolitanus (ad quem omnis et omnimoda jurisdictio spiritualis et ecclesiastica que ad episcopum ... sede plena pertinuit ipsa sede iam vacante notorie dignoscitur pertinere)*
> ..., by divine providence, Archbishop of Canterbury, Primate and Metropolitan of All England (to whom is commonly perceived to pertain all and all manner of jurisdiction, spiritual and ecclesiastical, which pertained to the Bishop of ... when that see was occupied [literally, "the seat being full"], that see now being vacant),
> *dilecto nobis in χριστο ... literato mandatorio nostro jurato*
> sends greeting to our beloved in Christ, ..., our sworn learned mandatary,
> *necnon universis et singulis clericis et literatis quibuscumque in et per totam diocesem ... predictum ubilibet constitutis salutem*
> and indeed to all and singular our clerks and learned men whomsoever in and throughout the whole diocese of ... aforesaid wherever constituted.
> *Vobis coniunctim et divisim precipimus et firmiter injungendo mandamus quatenus citetis seu citari faciatis peremptorie ... de ... in comitatu et diocese ... viduam relictam et administratricem bonorum jurium et creditorum ... nuper de eadem mercatoris defuncti*
> We warn and order you, jointly and severally, firmly enjoining you, that you should peremptorily cite or cause to be cited ..., of ... in the county and diocese of ..., widow, the relict and administratrix of the goods, rights and credits of ..., late of the same, merchant, deceased,
> *quod compareat coram nobis Vicario nostro in Spiritualibus Generali ejusve Surrogato aut alio Judice hac in parte competenti quocumque in Ecclesia Cathedrali ... locoque consistoriali episcopali ibidem die Jovis scilicet ... die mensis ... proxime futuro hora [audientarum often omitted] causarum ad iura ibidem reddenda consueta*
> that she should appear before us, our Vicar General in Spiritualities, or our surrogate, or any other judge whomsoever competent in this regard, in the cathedral church of ... and in the episcopal consistory in the same place, on Thursday, that is to say, the ... day of the month of ... next in the future, at the customary hour of hearing causes for law to be given in the same place,

inventarium verum plenum et particulare omnium et singulorum bonorum jurium et creditorum dicti defuncti que citra ejus mortem ad manus notitiam sive possessionem suas quoquomodo pervenerint nec non computum calculum sive ratiocinium de et super administratione sua in vim juramenti sui corporalis exhibitura et redditura
to exhibit and render, upon the strength of her corporal oath, a true, full and detailed inventory of all and singular the goods, rights and credits of the said deceased which may since his death, in any way whatsoever, have come to her hands, notice or possession, and indeed an account, calculation or reckoning of and upon her administration,

ulteriusque factura et receptura quod justam fuerit in hac parte ad voluntariam promotionem ... generosi principalis creditoris dicti defuncti
and further to do and suffer that which shall be just in this regard, at the voluntary motion of ..., gentleman, the principal creditor of the said deceased.

Et quid in premissis feceritis nos Vicarium nostrum in Spiritualibus Generalem predictum ejusve surrogatum aut alium judicem in hac parte competentem quemcumque debite certificetis unacum presentibus
And that which you do in the premises you should duly certify to us, our aforesaid Vicar General in Spiritualities, or our surrogate, or any other judge whomsoever competent in this regard, together with these presents.

Data sub sigillo officii nostri quo in hac parte utimur ... die mensis ... anno domini ...
Given under the seal of our office which we use in this regard on the ... day of the month of ... in the ... year of our Lord.

Similarly a citation might have been necessary simply to start the ball rolling and get someone to accept or renounce administration;

Quod compareat coram nobis ...
That he/she should appear before us etc

Litteras administrationis bonorum jurium creditorum et chattallorum dicti ... defuncti in se acceptatura/us vel refutatura/us vel aliter renunciatura/us
to take upon him/herself Letters of Administration of the goods, rights, credits and chattels of the said ... deceased, or to refute or otherwise to renounce them, [The ending of the future participles will agree with the gender and number of subjects of the citation]

alioquin causam rationabilem et legitimam si quam pro sese habeat aut dicere queat/queant
or otherwise to state reasonable and lawful cause, if such he/she/they has/have, or is/are able to say

quare Littere Administrationis bonorum jurium et creditorum ejusdem defuncti cum ejus testamento annexo si quod condiderit vel aliter simpliciter credit ... creditori principali ejusdem defuncti committi et concedi non debeant
why he/she believes Letters of Administration of the goods, rights, credits of the same deceased, with his will annexed if he made one, or otherwise alone, ought not to be committed and granted to ... principal creditor of the same deceased.

INTERROGATORIES

The probate process did not always go smoothly. A will might go missing, be disputed, or be deficient in some way. The court would then need to take statements (depositions) from people (deponents) who knew the deceased and his intentions, especially those present when he made his will. The genealogical content of these statements is often greater than that of a will, as they usually begin with a description of the deponent; his name, age, parish of birth, parish of present residence, and length of abode in the present parish.

A similar inquiry may be held if the deceased had had no time to make a written will but made a nuncupative will on his death bed. Obviously the court had to watch out for fraud, but if there was no dispute, and the estate was going to the wife and children, there was usually no difficulty in getting probate.

Where there was a dispute each side produced witnesses and also compiled a list of questions to be asked of the witnesses produced by the other side. The responses were considered by the judge, who would give his decision in the form of a Definitive Sentence or Final Decree.

The list of questions was known as an interrogatory and the replies made up the deposition. The interrogatories and depositions were usually in English with perhaps just a little Latin at the beginning and end. If you are unlucky, however, the whole proceedings may be recorded in Latin. The following example is typical of the records held in Canterbury Cathedral Archives;

> *In dei nomine Amen*
> In the name of God, Amen,
>> *coram vobis venerabili viro Magistro ... legum doctore Reverendissimi patris ac domini domini ... divina permissione Cantuariensis Archiepiscopi totius Anglie primatus et metropolitani ad causas ecclesiasticas in et per totam civitatem et diocesem Cantuariensem audiendum finiendum et determinandum commissario specialiter deputato patrone in hac parte surrogato aut alio judice in hac parte competenti quocumque*
>> before you, the worshipful Master ..., Doctor of Laws, Commissary, specially deputed, of the most reverend father and Lord in Christ ..., by divine permission, Lord Archbishop of Canterbury, Primate and Metropolitan of all England, for hearing, ending and determining ecclesiastical causes in and throughout the whole city and diocese of Canterbury, [or before your] patron in this regard, [your] Surrogate, or any other judge whomsoever competent in this regard,

You might think "of Canterbury" ought to be *Cantuarie* but these ecclesiastical titles are in the nature of adjectives; the "Canterburian" Archbishop, Diocese etc.

Pars honeste mulieris ... contra et adversus ... de eadem ac contra quemcumque alium coram vobis in iuditio pro eodem legitime intervenientem per viam querele ac vobis in hac parte querelentem dicit allegat et in his scriptis in iure proponit articulatim prout sequitur

The party of the honest woman ... against and adverse to ... of the same, and against any other person whomsoever lawfully intervening in justice for the same, by way of complaint, and complaining to you in this regard, says, alleges, and in these writings puts forward in law, article by article, just as follows;

Interrogatoria ministrata et iurata ex parte et per partem ... dum vixit parochie de ... defuncti quibuscumque testibus pretensis contra omnes et singulos testes pretensos ex parte et per partem ... relicte dicti defuncti et pretense executricis asserte testamenti sive ultime voluntatis defuncti in quadam pretensa causa diffamacionis productos et producendos sequuntur videlicet

The interrogatories administered and sworn on behalf of and by the party of ... while he lived of the parish of ... deceased, to whomsoever the pretended witnesses produced and to be produced against all and singular the witnesses on behalf of and by the party of ... the relict of the said deceased and the pretended and asserted executrix of the testament or last will of the deceased, in a certain pretended cause of defamation, follow, that is to say;

Imprimis videlicet petit pars dicti ... quod exponatur eis et eorum cuilibet predictorum testium periculum periurii et pena falsidici testis et quod tunc interrogabuntur de eius ætate arte condicione mora et ortu suis et quamdiu noverunt partes litigantes in hac causa.

First, that is to say, the party of the said ... asks that there should be explained to them, and to each one of them of the aforesaid witnesses, the danger of perjury and the penalty of bearing false witness, and that they shall then be asked concerning their age, occupation, condition, residence and origin, and how long they have known the parties litigant in this cause.

Et interrogabuntur coniunctim divisim et de quolibet.

And they shall be asked jointly, severally, and each for himself.

Item interrogetur quilibet testis huiusmodi ad cuius seu quorum instanciam, motum seu requisicionem venit in hac parte testificatur

Item each witness should be asked this; at whose [singular and plural] instance, motion or request does he come and testify in this regard?

Et interrogentur coniunctim divisim et de quolibet

And they should be asked jointly, severally, and each for himself.

Item interrogetur quilibet huiusmodi pretensus testis testium an sit consanguineus vel affinis parti/s eum producenti/s et si dicat quod sic tunc interrogetur in quo gradu consanguinitatis seu affinitatis sit ei coniunctus seu connexus Et interrogabuntur ut supra

Item each pretended witness of the witnesses should be asked this; whether he is a kinsman or relation to/of the party producing him, and if he should say that he is such, then he should be asked in what degree of kinship or affinity he is joined or connected to him. And they shall be asked as above [ie jointly, severally, and each for himself].

... de ... in comitatu ... yeoman ubi moram fecit per totam vitam suam ibidem natus/ortus etatis sexaginti annorum aut eo circiter testis iuratus deponit ut sequitur

... of ... in the county of ... yeoman, where he has lived for all his life, born/originating in the same place, of the age of sixty years or thereabouts, a sworn witness, deposes as follows

Ad primam allegacionem et schedulam testamentariam huiusmodi deponit

To the first allegation and testamentary schedule he deposes

Ad 2, 3, 4, 5 et 6^{tum} articulos iste deponens dicit

To the 2nd, 3rd, 4th, 5th and 6th articles this deponent says

Et reddit racionem scientie sue in predepositis huiusmodi

And he gives the reason of his knowledge in these before-deposed matters.

Et aliter nescit deponere sed refert se ad iuramentum

And otherwise he knows not how to depose, but refers himself to / reminds himself of his oath.

Ad ultimam dicit predeposita per eum fuisse et esse vera etc

To the last he says the things before-deposed by him were and are true etc [literally, "he says them to have been and to be true etc"].

DEFINITIVE SENTENCE OR FINAL DECREE

Occasionally it would happen that there was a dispute over a will. A potential beneficiary might have believed that the testator had been coerced into making his will in a particular manner, or into nominating a particular executor. He might have thought that the executor was acting unlawfully, or behaving unreasonably, by unnecessarily prolonging the administration for example. In the case of an intestacy he might have felt that administration had been committed to an unsuitable person. His remedy was to ask the court to review the case and make a pronouncement upon its findings. This is known as a "Definitive Sentence or Final Decree".

As regards translation, if you are not familiar with the "ablative absolute" construction before you start, you will be by the time you finish! This is a way of inserting words into a sentence so that they stay outside the main action.

The underlying theme of a definitive sentence is simple: "We, the judge, have decided to make this decree." (The judge uses an ecclesiastical version of the majestic plural.) He wants to make it clear that he has considered all the points of view so he starts by saying, "The merits and circumstances having been heard, viewed and discussed by us …" The words *meritis, circumstanciis, auditis, visis* and *discussis* form an ablative absolute and are in the ablative case accordingly.

Similarly, while the judge is reviewing the case, the parties stand on the sidelines hoping for judgment in their favour, so we get more ablative absolutes; the parties appearing, *partibus comparentibus*, and *parte postulante et petente*, the party beseeching and seeking, for example.

His decision made, (another ablative absolute there!), the judge tells us that the proceedings so far having been scrutinised and reviewed, *processu rimato et recensito*, and everything which was to be observed having in fact been observed, *servatis servandis*, (yet more ablative absolutes) he has decided to proceed.

And after all the background, the verb *duximus* finally provides the subject of the sentence (the grammatical sentence that is, not the legal one); "we". The word *nos* has appeared before of course, but only in the context of *per nos*, by us.

Sententia pro valore/confirmacione testamenti … defuncti
Sentence for/ as to the validity/confirmation of the testament of … deceased
Sententia absolutoria ex parte … contra …
Absolutory sentence on behalf of … against …

In dei nomine amen
In the name of God, Amen,

Auditis visis et intellectis ac/et plenarie et mature discussis per nos ... militem et Legum Doctorem Curie Prerogative Cantuariensis Magistrum Custodem sive Commissarium legitime constitutum/deputatum meritis et circumstanciis cuiusdam negotii/cause testamentarie sive probacionis testamenti sive ultime voluntatis ...
The merits and circumstances of a certain matter / testamentary cause, or [matter] of the probate of the testament or last will of ... [A], having been heard, viewed and considered, and fully and opportunely/maturely investigated, by us, ..., Doctor of Laws, Master, Keeper or Commissary, lawfully constituted/deputed, of the Prerogative Court of Canterbury,

Something like this may appear at the point marked [A] above;

[A] *cuiusdam ... nuper dum vixit parochie ... in comitatu ...*
of a certain ..., late, while he lived, of the parish of ... in the county of ...
defuncti habentis dum vixit et mortis sue tempore bona jura sive credita in diversis diocesibus sive peculiaribus jurisdictionibus provincie Cantuariensis sufficientia ad fundandum jurisdictionem Curie Prerogative Cantuariensis predicte
deceased [I prefer to say "who died"] having, while he lived and at the time of his death, goods, rights or credits in diverse dioceses or peculiar jurisdictions of the province of Canterbury sufficient to found the jurisdiction of the Prerogative Court of Canterbury aforesaid
et probacionis eiusdem testamenti sive ultime voluntatis per testes
and of the probate of the same testament or last will by the witnesses

Somewhere round here you need to insert the phrase, "proceeding correctly and lawfully" or "rightly and duly proceeding" although the equivalent Latin only appears much farther down, at [C] below. Sometimes the clerk writes *procedentes* [plural] in which case he must be telling us that the judge [*nos*] was proceeding lawfully. Sometimes he writes *procedens* [singular] which may simply indicate a "confusion of number", but may also mean that it is the matter which is proceeding. And sometimes he writes *proceden'* leaving you to decide.

Que/Quod coram nobis in judicio
Which cause/matter [*que* (feminine) if the point at issue is a cause (*causa*); *quod* (neuter) if it is a matter or business (*negotium*)] [was] before us in judgment, [from [B] below] for some time, unsettled, and still is unsettled and standing undecided,
inter ... executorem/executricem testamenti sive ultime voluntatis dicti defuncti
between ... the executor/executrix of the testament or last will of the said deceased [or some similar description]
partem agentem et huiusmodi negotium promoventem ex una
the party acting and moving this matter, on the one [side]
Et dictum ...
And the said ...,
executorem in testamento dicti ... nominatum et constitutum
the executor named and constituted in the testament of the said ...

administratorem pretensum bonorum jurium et creditorum dicti defuncti
the pretended/claimed administrator of the goods, rights and credits of the said deceased
partem ream / appelatam et querelatam
the party defendant / appealed against / complained against
contra quam hoc/idem negotio promovetur
against whom this/the same matter is moved,
parte/partibus ex altera in specie
the party/parties on the other [side], in particular,
ac omnes alios in genere ius titulum aut interesse in dicto testamento sive ultima voluntate aut bonis juribus catallis seu creditis dicti defuncti in hac parte habentes seu habere pretendentes
And all others in general having or pretending/claiming to have right, title or interest in the said testament or last will, or in the goods, rights, chattels or credits, of the said deceased,
[B] *nuper/aliquandiu iudicialiter controvertebatur/vertebatur et pendebat adhuc vertitur(que) et pendet indecisa/um*
[see above] was before us in judgment lately/for some time, being considered, and [still] is being considered, and pending/standing undecided/unsettled,
[C] *rite et legitime procedentes* [see above]

partibus predictis per earum respective procuratores legitime constitutos coram nobis in judicio legitime comparentibus
the parties aforesaid, through their respective lawfully constituted proctors, appearing lawfully before us in judgment,
parteque dicti/prefati/antedicti ... per procuratorem suum legitimum coram nobis comparente sententiam postulante et petente ferri et justiciam fieri pro parte sua
and the party of the said/aforenamed/beforesaid ... appearing before us through his lawful proctor, seeking and beseeching [sometimes the "seeking and beseeching" has to be imported from the next paragraph] sentence to be carried out, and justice to be done, for [or "on behalf of" or "in favour of"] his/her/their party,
parteque/partibusque vero etiam antedicti/prefati/memorati ... per procuratorem suum similiter respective comparente/comparentibus instanter postulante et petente / postulantibus et petentibus sententiam ferri et justiciam fieri pro parte sua
and indeed the party of the beforesaid/aforenamed/before-mentioned ... through his/her/their proctor similarly respectively appearing and vehemently seeking and beseeching sentence to be carried out, and justice to be done, for his/her/their party,
ceteris vero partibus prenominatis omnibus et singulis tam in specie quam in genere citatis intimatis ac preconizatis et non comparentibus sed contumaciter sese absentantibus
and indeed all and singular the rest of the parties beforenamed, both in particular and in general, having been cited, given intimation and forewarned, and not appearing, but contumaciously absenting themselves,
rimatoque primitus per nos toto et integro processu alias/coram nobis in hac/hoc/huiusmodi causa/negotio habito et facto ac/atque diligenter recensito

and all and the whole proceedings had and done at another time/before us in this matter/cause having been first scrutinised and diligently reviewed by us,
servatisque per nos de jure in hac parte servandis
and those things in this regard which are by law to be observed [*servandis*] having been observed [*servatis*] by us,

We have thus decided / thought fit [*sic duximus* from [D] below]
ad nostre sententie diffinitive sive nostri finalis decreti prolacionem in huiusmodi negotio ferendum
to carry out [*ad ferendum*] the publication of our definitive sentence or final decree in this matter,
in presentia partis prefati …
in the presence of the party of the aforenamed …
et in penam contumacionis predictorum omnium et singulorum aliorum tam in specie quam in genere citatorum intimatorum ac preconizatorum et non comparentium
and in pain of the contumacy of all and singular aforesaid others, both in particular and in general, cited, given intimation and forewarned, and not appearing
[D] *sic duximus procedendum fore et procedimus in hunc qui sequitur modum*
[and this is] to be proceeded with, and we do thus proceed, in this manner, which follows.

Quia per acta inactitata deducta allegata exhibita proposita probata pariter et confessata in huiusmodi/hoc/isto negotio comperimus et luculenter invenimus
Whereas / Forasmuch as by the acts enacted, led out, alleged, exhibited, propounded, and equally proved and acknowledged in this matter, we have well concluded and found
partem prefati/memorati … intencionem suam
the party of the aforenamed/before-mentioned …, [and] his argument
in quadam/quibusdam allegacione et testamento/schedula/compoto alias coram nobis ex parte dicti … datis exhibitis et admissis
set out / led out [*deductam* [E] below] in a certain allegation and testament/schedule/account given, exhibited and admitted before us at another time on behalf of the said …,
et penes registrum huius curiæ remanente/ibus [agreeing the number of items exhibited] [E] *deductam* [agreeing *intencionem*]
and remaining in the possession of the registrar of this court,
cuius quidem allegacionis tenor sequitur et est talis videlicet
of which allegation, indeed, the tenor follows, and is such, that is to say:

Beware the word *quidem*. It is often translated as "a certain". Thus *cuius quidem allegacionis*; "of which certain allegation". This confuses *quidem* with *quidam*. In fact *quidem*, like *vero*, is indeclinable and means "indeed". If the clerk had meant "of which certain", he should have written *cuiusdam*. Of course, the clerk might think one thing and custom and practice might impel him to write another.

Here the opening words of the libel, allegation, or whatever the document originating the action was, may be repeated, presumably so that the correct one can be identified and linked up later if necessary. For example;

> *Quo die / Deinde ... nomine procuratorii ac ut procurator legitimus dicti ... exhibuit testamentum originale dicti defuncti*
> On which day / Then ..., in the name of his proxy [ie procuracy], and as lawful proctor of the said ... exhibited the original testament of the said
> *et allegavit dictum defunctum mentis compotem et in sua sana memoria existentem illud suum testamentum suam in se continens ultimam voluntatem condidisse fecisse et declarasse*
> and alleged the said deceased, being whole of mind and in his healthy memory, to have composed, made, and declared that his testament, containing in it [his] last will

The main thrust of the decision is then resumed.

> *Quam/Que/Quos quidem allegacionem et testamentum pro hic lecta/lectam et inserta/insertam habemus et haberi volumus*
> Which allegation and testament, indeed, having been read and taken into account for this purpose, we hold, and wish it to be held, [hold/held reads better than have/had] [*lectis* and *insertis* often appear here too although they should be in the accusative case]
> *sufficienter et ad plenum fundasse pariter et probasse*
> to have been sufficiently and to the fullest founded, and equally proved,
> *minus sufficienter fundasse aut probasse sed in probacione eiusdem penitus omnino defecisse et deficere*
> [or alternatively] to have been less than sufficiently founded or proved, but to have been utterly deficient, and to be utterly deficient, in proof of the same,
> *quoad infra/inferius per nos pronunciandum*
> so far as is to be pronounced by us within/below,
> *Nihilque saltem effectuale ex parte aut/et per partem antedicti ... in hoc negotio / in hac parte fuisse aut esse deductum exceptum allegatum exhibitum propositum probatum aut confessatum fuisse aut esse in hac parte*
> And [we have found] nothing, at least [nothing] of any effect, to have been or to be put forward, excepted, alleged, exhibited, propounded, proved or acknowledged in this matter / in this regard by and/or one behalf of the party of the beforesaid ...
> *quod intentionem partis prefati ... elideret seu quomodolibet enervaret*
> which in any way destroyed or weakened the argument of the aforenamed ... in this regard.

> *Idcirco nos ... Legum Doctor Judex antedictus Χριστι/Christi nomine primitus invocato ac ipsum solum deum oculis nostris preponentes et habentes*
> For that reason we, ... Doctor of Laws, the Judge beforesaid, the name of Christ having first been invoked, and putting and having him, God, alone before our eyes,
> *de/deque et cum consilio jurisperitorum cum quibus in hac parte communicavimus matureque deliberavimus*
> and by and with the advice of those people, learned in the law, with whom we have communicated and opportunely deliberated in this regard,

Pronounce decree and declare; [From [F] below. In the best Latin tradition, these verbs occur at the end of the sentence, but the sentence may extend over several paragraphs.]

The nature of the judge's decision will depend on the nature of the point at issue. He may decide that the will is void, the executor is acting rightfully, or that one of the parties should be absolved and dismissed, for example. Whatever the decision, the "accusative and infinitive" construction is used. The judge considers such-a-body (accusative) to have done/made (infinitive) such-a-thing, and administration (accusative) to be committed (infinitive), etc etc. The following sections are typical.

Confirmation of a Will

> *prenominatum … defunctum dum vixit compotem mentis et in sua sana et perfecta memoria existentem dictum suum testamentum sive ultimam voluntatem suam in scriptis rite et legitime fecisse condidisse et declarasse*
> the beforenamed … deceased, while he lived, being whole of mind and in his healthy and perfect memory, to have correctly and lawfully made, composed and declared his said testament or last will in writing,
> *ac/atque in eodem sive eadem prefatum/prefatam … dicti sui testamenti sive ultime voluntatis nominasse ordinasse fecisse ac constituisse executorem/executricem*
> and in the same to have named, ordained, made and constituted the aforenamed … as executor/executrix of his said testament or last will,
> *ceteraque/omniaque et singula fecisse voluisse legasse donasse dedisse reliquisse et disposuisse in omnibus et per omnia* [*pro omnia* also often appears, even though *pro* governs the ablative] *prout in dicto/eodem testamento sive ultima voluntate sic ut prefertur modo exhibito ac penes Registrum huius Curie remanente continetur*
> and to have done, willed, bequeathed, donated, given, left and disposed all and singular other / the rest [of his affairs] in and through all things just as is contained in the said/same testament or last will, now, just as is aforesaid, exhibited, and remaining in the possession of the registrar of this court
> *quodque idem dictum testamentum fuit et erat in vita dicti testatoris (atque de eius mandato) in scriptis redactum et conceptum*
> and that the same said testament had been and was, in the lifetime of the said testator (and by his order) conceived and rendered in/into writing,
> *et coram eodem palam et publice perlectum et recitatum*
> and before him openly and publicly read over and recited,
> *ac per eundem testatorem manu et sigillo suis propriis subscriptum et sigillatum*
> and subscribed and sealed by the same testator with his own hand and seal,
> *proque suo vero testamento et sive ultima voluntate in presentiis nonnullorum testium fidedignorum fassum recognitum approbatum et ratificatum*
> and acknowledged, recognised, approved and ratified as/to be/for his true testament and or last will in the presence of not a few trustworthy witnesses

et post scripturam eiusdem testamentum huiusmodi sigillo suo sigillasse nomenque suum manu sua propria subscripsisse
and after the writing of this same testament, to have sealed it with his seal and to have subscribed his name with his own hand

et hoc facto testamentum sive ultimam voluntatem huiusmodi coram nonnullis testibus fidedignis recognovisse confirmasse tradidisse et publicasse
and this having been done, to have recognised, confirmed, handed over and published this testament or last will before not a few trustworthy witnesses

proque viribus valore et validitate eiusdem testamenti ut prefertur exhibiti et allegati
and [we pronounce, decree and declare] as to the force, worth and validity of the aforesaid testament, exhibited and alleged as is aforesaid.

[F] *pronunciamus decernimus et declaramus* [see above]

Nullity / Letters of Administration

Prefatum ... defunctum ab hac luce nullo per eum condito testamento migrasse
[We pronounce, perceive and declare] the aforenamed ... deceased to have departed from this light [I prefer "departed this life"], no testament having been made by him,

Litteras igitur pretensas administrationis bonorum dicti ... defuncti alias prefato ... per nos commissas et concessas cassamus irritamus et annullamus ac pro nullis et invalidis ad omnem iuris effectum tenemus
[And] therefore we quash, void and annul the pretended Letters of Administration of the goods of the said ... deceased committed and granted by us to the aforenamed ... at another time, and hold them as null and invalid to all effect of law

Administrationemque omnium et singulorum bonorum jurium et creditorum dictum defunctum et suum huiusmodi testamentum qualitercumque concernentium executori unico in eodem nominato committendam esse pronunciamus atque committimus
And we pronounce and commit administration of all and singular the goods, rights and credits in any way whatsoever concerning the said deceased and this his testament to be committed to the sole executor named in the same.

Absolution

Prenominatos ... ab instancia et impeticione dicti ... quoad deducta narrata petita et proposita ex parte eiusdem ... et ulteriori judicii observacione dimittendos et absolvendos fore de iure debere pronunciamus decernimus et declaramus sicque cum effectu absolvimus et dimittimus
We pronounce, perceive and declare [that] the aforenamed ... ought to be dismissed and absolved in law from the instance and accusation of the said ... so far as concerns the matters led out, narrated, sought and propounded/proposed on behalf of the same ... and from any further judicial observance, and we do thus, with effect, absolve and dismiss them.

Dictumque ... in expensis legitimis ex parte et per partem prefati ... in hac parte factis et faciendis condemnandum fore de iure debere insuper pronunciamus et condemnamus per hanc nostram sententiam diffinitivam sive hoc nostrum finale decretum quam sive quod ferimus et promulgamus in hiis scriptis

And moreover by this our definitive sentence or final decree, which we carry out and publish in these writings, we pronounce and condemn [that] the said … ought to be condemned in law in the legitimate expenses incurred and to be incurred in this regard on behalf of and by the party of the aforenamed …

Taxacionem vero sive moderacionem expensarum huiusmodi nobis nostrove surrogato aut alii iudici in hac parte competenti cuicumque reservandam et reservamus
Taxation, indeed, or moderation, of these expenses is to be reserved, and we do reserve it, to us or our surrogate, or to any other judge whomsoever competent in this regard.

Lecta lata et promulgata fuit hec sententia diffinitiva per dictum Magistrum … legum doctorem Curie Prerogative Cantuariensis Magistrum Custodem sive Commissarium legitime constitutum
This definitive sentence was read, carried out and published by the said Master …, Doctor of Laws, Master, Keeper or Commissary lawfully constituted, of the Prerogative Court of Canterbury,
… die judicio/juridico post festum sive diem sancti … die Jovis … videlicet mensis … anno domini … inter horas nonam et undecimam ante meridiem / primam et quintam post meridiem illius diei
on the … law day after the feast or day of Saint … on Thursday, that is to say, the … day of the month of … in the … year of our Lord, between the ninth and eleventh hours before noon / the first and fifth hours after noon of that day,
in Aula communi Hospitii dominorum Advocatorum Curie Cantuariensis de Arcubus London / in Edibus suis / in Consistoria / loco Consistoriali infra Ecclesiam Cathedralem Sancti/Divi Pauli London judicialiter et pro tribunali sedentem
sitting judicially and as a tribunal in the common hall of the lodgings of the Lords Advocate of the Court of Arches of Canterbury in London / in his rooms/house / in the consistory within the Cathedral Church of Saint Paul in London
ad petitionem Magistri … Notarii Publici Procuratoris originalis supranominati …
at the petition of Master …, notary public, original proctor of the abovenamed …
ac in presentia …
and in the presence of …
necnon in penam contumaciæ tam prefatorum … in specie quam omnium et singulorum aliorum ius titulum aut interesse in testamento vel bonis dicti defuncti habentium seu habere pretendentium in genere sic ut prefertur citatorum intimatorum et preconizatorum et non comparentium sed sese contumaciter absentantium
and indeed in the pain of contumacy of both the aforesaid … in particular, and of all and singular others in general having or pretending/claiming to have right, title or interest in the testament or goods of the said deceased, thus, as is aforesaid, cited, given intimation and forewarned, and not appearing, but contumaciously absenting themselves
super cuius sententie prolationem idem/dictus Magister … requisivit me … Notarium Publicum dicte Curie Registrarii Deputatum tunc et ibidem presentem conficere / ad conficiendum sibi unum vel plura instrumentum seu instrumenta publica exinde

upon pronouncement of which sentence the same/said Master ... asked/required me, ..., Notary Public, Deputy of the Registrar of the said Court, being then and there present, to make for him one or more public instruments in repect thereof
ac testes inferius nominatos eorum testimonium de super perhibere
and to call the witnesses named below [to give] their testimony thereupon.
Presentibus tunc et ibidem
Then and there present;
venerabilibus viris ... et ... dicte curie advocatis
the worshipful [men] ... and ..., advocates of the said court
necnon Magistris ... et ... legum doctoribus Notariis Publicis dicte curie procuratoribus testibus super prolatione sententie prædicte
and indeed Masters ... and ..., Doctors of Law, Notaries Public, proctors of the said court, witnesses upon the putting forward of the aforesaid sentence.
Examinatur
It is examined.

Although I have referred above specifically to testamentary causes, a definitive sentence might be the conclusion to anything that concerned the church courts, for example defamation.

EXCOMMUNICATION

One of the standard clauses in a Definitive Sentence refers to the pain of contumacy, ie the penalty for disobedience. The ultimate penalty was excommunication. This punishment might be considered appropriate in all sorts of ecclesiastical causes, not just testamentary ones; fornication and adultery, for example. The order might include clauses similar to the following.

> *In Dei nomine Amen*
> In the name of God, Amen,
>> ... *vicarius in spiritualibus generalis reverendi in christo/χριστο patris ac domini domini ... providencia/permissione divina ... episcopi curieque consistorialis episcopalis ... predicti officialis principalis*
>> ..., Vicar General in Spiritualities of the Reverend Father and Lord in Christ, ..., by divine providence/permission Lord Bishop of ..., and Official Principal of the Consistory Court of the Bishop of ... aforesaid,
>> *universis et singulis rectoribus vicariis capellanis clericis curatis et literatis ministris quibuscumque infra in et per totam diocesem nostram / totum archidiaconatum nostrum ubilibet constitutis Salutem in Domino*
>> [sends] greeting in the lord to all and singular rectors, vicars, chaplains, clerks, curates and learned ministers whomsoever, in and throughout our whole diocese / our whole archdeaconry, wherever constituted.
>> *Cum venerabilis vir ... Legum Doctor supreme Curie Cancellarie Anglie Magistrorum unus rite et legitime procedens*
>> Whereas the worshipful man ..., Doctor of Laws, one of the Masters of the Supreme Court of the Chancery of England, proceeding correctly and lawfully
>> *Cum nos in quibusdam separalibus causis subtractionis rate sive ratarum erga reparacionem ecclesie parochialis de ... in comitatu et archidiaconatu ... quæ coram nobis in iudicio*
>> Whereas we, in certain separate causes of underpayment of the rate or rates towards the reparation of the parish church of ... in the county and archdeaconry of ... which was before us in judgment
>> *Quia nos in iudicio rite et legitime procedentes in quodam negotio officii nostri quod coram nobis in iudicio inter ... partem agentem et querelentem ex una*
>> Because we, correctly and lawfully proceeding in judgment in a certain matter of our office which was before us in judgment between ..., the party moving and complaining, on the one [side],
>> *et contra ... de ... in comitatu predicto ... partem ream et querelatam partem ex altera*
>> and against ... of ... in the county aforesaid, the party defendant and complained against, on the other [side],
>> *aliquandiu vertebatur vertiturque et pendet adhuc indecisum*
>> [which matter] was being considered for some time, and still is being considered, and pending/standing undecided/unsettled,

quendam ... de parochia de ... diocesis ... propter eius manifestam contumacionem in non comparendo coram eo certis hora et loco competenter sibi assignatis iam effluxis in quodam negotio contribucionis ad reparacionem et usum ecclesie parochialis de ... predicto de iusticia responsurum alias legitime et peremptorie citatum sepius et publice preconizatum diuque et sufficienter expectatum et nullo modo comparentem pronuntiaverit contumacem

[He] has pronounced a certain ... of the parish of ... in [literally "of"] the diocese of ... [to be] contumacious, on account of his manifest contumacy in not appearing before him at a certain hour and place, competently/properly assigned to him [and] now expired, to answer to justice at another time in a certain matter of contribution to the repair and use of the parish church of ... aforesaid, he having been lawfully and peremptorily cited, and often and publicly forewarned, and for a long and sufficient time awaited, and in no way appearing,

et in penam contumacionis sue huiusmodi excommunicandum fore decreverit

and decreed him, in penalty of this his contumacy, to be excommunicated.

Nos igitur ... clericus sufficienti auctoritate in hac parte fulcitus dictum ... in hiis scriptis excommunicamus

Now therefore we ..., clerk, founded by sufficient authority in this regard, excommunicate the said ... in these writings.

Eosdem ... et ... propter eorum respective contumacias in non comparendo coram nobis certis die hora et Loco eis respective prefixis jamque effluxis/elapsis alias rite legitime et peremptorie citatis iuxta citacionem eis factam trina/3na vice preconizatis diuque et sufficienter expectatis et nullo modo comparentibus sed sese contumaciter absentantibus pronunciavimus contumaces

We have pronounced the same ... and ... contumacious on account of their respective contumacies in not appearing before us, according to the summons made to them, at a certain date, hour and place respectively pre-appointed to them, and now passed, and they having been correctly, lawfully and peremptorily summoned at another time, and three times warned, and long and sufficiently awaited, and in no way appearing, but wilfully absenting themselves,

et in penam contumaciarum suarum huiusmodi excommunicandos fore decrevimus ad peticionem partis antedicti ... justitia mediante

and, justice mediating, and in penalty of their contumacies, we have decreed them to be excommunicated, at the petition of the party of the beforesaid ...

Cumque dilectus noster Reverendus vir ... clericus et presbyter auctoritate sufficienti in ea parte fulcitus eosdem ... et ... propter manifestas suas respectivas in premissis contumacias hujusmodi (sic ut premittitur) iuxta decretum antedictum ex prescripto nostro excommunicavit in scriptis per cum lectum justitia id poscens

And whereas our beloved Reverend ..., Clerk and Priest, founded by sufficient authority in that regard, has, by our order, excommunicated the same ... and ... on account of these, their respective manifest contumacies in the premises, (just as is aforesaid), according to the beforesaid decree in writing read by him, justice demanding it

vobis igitur conjunctim et divisim committimus ac firmiter injungendo mandamus quatenus prefatos ... et ... auctoritate nostra propter contumacias suas hujusmodi excommunicatos fuisse et esse et pro personis excommunicatis in ecclesiis vestris parochialibus et presertim in ecclesia parochiali de ... die aliquo dominico seu festivo diebus Dominicalis seu Festivis proxime sequentibus post receptionem presentium palam et publice denuncietis et declaretis seu sic denuntiari et declarari facietis cum effectu

therefore we commit to you, jointly and severally, and firmly enjoining you we order, that you should, in your parish churches, and especially in the parish church of ..., on any Sunday/Sundays or Feast Day/Days next following after the receipt of these presents, by our authority, openly and publicly denounce and declare, or cause it thus to be denounced and declared, with effect that the aforenamed ... and ... have been and are excommunicated

The previous sentence may also include one of the following phrases;

divinorum temporibus dum major in eisdem adfuerit populi multitudo
at the times of divine services while the greater part of the people are present in the same
ibidem ad divina audienda adfuerit populi multitudo
[when] a congregation of the people is present in the same place to hear divine services,

Et quid in premissis feceritis nos nostrumve surrogatum nostrum legitimum aut alium judicem in hac parte competentem quemcumque unacum presentibus debite certificetis
And that which you may do in the premises you should duly certify, together with these presents, to us or our lawful surrogate or any other judge whomsoever competent in this regard.

The certificate referred to above may be included;

Excommunicatio hec denuntiata fuit in ecclesia parochiali de ... per me ... ... die ... anno salutis ...
This excommunication was denounced in the parish church of ... by me, ..., on the ... day of ... in the year of health ...

Sometimes a number of excommunications were carried out at once, as in this example from Kent;

In Dei nomine Amen
In the name of God, Amen,
Nos ... legum doctor civitatis et diocesis Cantuariensis Commissarius Generalis legitime deputatus
We, ..., Doctor of Laws, Commissary General, lawfully deputed, of the city and diocese of Canterbury,
omnes et singulos quorum nomina et cognomina hic inferius respective scribuntur et recitantur propter eorum manifestam contumacionem in non comparendo coram nobis nec parendo monicionibus nostris iustis et legitimis pronuntiamus contumaces
pronounce contumacious all and singular those whose names and surnames are here below respectively written and recited, on account of their manifest contumacy in not appearing before us, and in not complying with our just and lawful warnings,

et in pena contumacionis suarum huiusmodi excommunicandos fore decrevimus et excommunicavimus in hiis scriptis
and we have decreed them to be excommunicated in penalty of this their contumacy, and in these writings we do excommunicate them.
Ita pronuntiamus ... Commissarius Cantuariensis
We thus pronounce ... Commissary of Canterbury

WRITS

The purpose of a writ was to delegate royal power so that private individuals could, for example, hold an inquiry, or examine witnesses in a Chancery Cause. In the latter case a writ, also known as a commission, of *dedimus potestatem* [we have given power] was issued:

Writ of Dedimus Potestatem

> *… dei gratia Anglie Scotie Francie et Hibernie Rex fidei defensor etc*
> … by the grace of God, of England, Scotland, France and Ireland, King, defender of the faith etc,
> *dilectis sibi … … generosis salutem*
> [sends] greeting to his beloved [subjects] … … gentlemen. [Four commissioners should be named, two chosen by each side in the dispute.]
> *Cum … querens quandam peticionem coram nobis in Cancellaria nostra versus … et … defendentes nuper exhibuerit*
> Whereas … plaintiff, has lately exhibited a certain petition before us in our Chancery, against … and …, defendants,
> *quodque eisdem defendentibus per breve nostrum nuper precipimus / preceperimus quod essent coram nobis in dicta Cancellaria nostra ad certum diem iam preteritum peticioni predicte responsuri*
> and whereas we lately, by our writ, warned the same defendants [*precipio* takes the dative] that they should be before us in our said Chancery, on a certain day now passed, to answer the aforesaid petition [*respondeo* likewise takes the dative],
> *sciatis quod nos de fidelitatibus et providis circumspeccionibus vestris plurimum confidentes*
> may you know that we, fully confident of your faithfulness and prudent circumspection,
> *dedimus vobis tribus vel duobus vestrum potestatem et authoritatem ipsos defendentes de et super materia peticionis predicte cuius tenorem vobis mittimus presentibus interclusum diligenter examinandi*
> have given to you, or three or two of you, power and authority diligently to examine [literally "of examining"] the same defendants concerning and upon the matters of the aforesaid petition, the tenor of which we send to you enclosed with these presents,
> *Et ideo vobis tribus vel duobus vestrum mandamus quod ad certos diem/dies et locum/loca quos ad hoc provideritis ad prefatos defendentes si commode ad vos laborare non possint accedatis*
> And therefore we command you, or three or two of you, at a certain date and place / dates and places, which you should provide for this purpose, to approach the aforenamed defendants, if they are not able to travel conveniently to you,
> *ac ipsos defendentes de et super materia peticionis predicte super sacramenta sua tactis per ipsos prius coram vobis tribus vel duobus vestrum sacrosanctis dei evangeliis corporaliter prestanda diligenter examinetis*

and you should diligently examine the same defendants, on their corporal oaths, which are first to be administered corporally before you, or three or two of you, God's holy gospels being touched by them, concerning and upon the matters of the aforesaid petition,

responcionesque dictorum defendentium peticioni predicte fiendas cuius tenorem vobis mittimus presentibus interclusum super sacramenta sua per sancta dei evangelia corporaliter prestanda aut placita sua super sacramenta sua aut absque sacramentis suis sive moraciones dictorum defendentium peticioni predicte fiendas debite et respective recipiendi

and duly and respectively to receive the responses of the said defendants to be made to the aforesaid petition, the tenor of which we send to you enclosed with these presents, upon their oaths, to be administered corporally upon God's holy gospels, or their pleas (either upon their oaths or without them), or the demurrers of the said defendants to be made to the aforesaid petition [or alternatively];

ac suas responciones super eisdem fiendas ut dicitur recipiatis et in scriptis in pargameno redigatis

and you should receive their responses to be made upon the same, as is aforesaid, and render them into writing on parchment,

et cum illas sic ceperitis eas/illas nobis in dictam Cancellariam nostram in Octabis/Quindena Pasche proxime futuro ubicunque tunc fuerit sub sigillis vestris trium vel duorum vestrum clausas distincte et aperte mittatis unacum tenore predicto et hoc brevi

and when you have thus taken them down, you should send them to us, distinctly and plainly made, in our said Chancery wherever it may then be, in the octave/quindene of Easter [or whatever] next coming, closed under your seals or those of three or two of you, together with the tenor aforesaid, and this writ,

Teste me/nobis ipso/ipsis apud Westmonasterium ... die ... Anno Regni nostri ...

Witnessed by me/us myself/ourselves at Westminster on the ... day of ... in the ... year of our reign.

It may already be clear at the time of issue that the person to be examined cannot travel, in which case the following paragraphs will appear:

Ac idem ... adeo impotens sui existat quod usque Westmonasterium ad diem illum absque maximo corporis sui periculo laborare non sufficit ut accepimus

And the same ... is so weak that he is unfit to travel to Westminster on that day without the greatest bodily danger, as we accept;

Nos statui ipsius ... pie compacientes atque de fidelitatibus et providiis circumspeccionibus vestris plenius confidentes dedimus vobis potestatem et auctoritatem ipsum ... de et super materia peticionis predicte diligenter examinandi responsionemque suam super eadem recipiendi et in scriptis redigendi

[May you know that we], dutifully compassionate to the state of the same ..., and fully confident of your faithfulness and prudent circumspection, have given you power and authority diligently to examine the same ... concerning and upon the matters of the aforesaid petition, and to receive his response upon the same, and to render it into writing.

Before granting certain liberties such as a fair or market, the crown would want to be sure that this was not to its own detriment. A writ of *ad quod dampnum* [to what damage] was sent to the appropriate Sheriff instructing him to inquire into the matter. Such a writ might also be issued if a crown tenant proposed to transfer land to the church, as a state of mortmain might ensue, with the crown losing the opportunity to profit from feudal dues such as heriots, wardships and escheats.

Writ for Inquisition ad quod Dampnum

Edwardus dei gratia Rex Anglie Dominus Hibernie et Dux Aquitanie vicecomiti Eboraci salutem

Edward, by the grace of God, King of England, Lord of Ireland, and Duke of Aquitaine, sends greetings to the Sheriff of York.

Precipimus/mandamus tibi quod per sacramentum proborum et legalium hominum de comitatu tuo per quos rei veritas melius sciri poterit diligenter inquiras si sit ad dampnum vel preiudicium nostrum aut aliorum si concedamus ... quod ipse tres acras terre et dimidiam et unam rodam prati cum pertinentiis in ... dare possit et assignare dilectis nobis in Christo Priori et Conventui ...

We order you that, (by the corporal oath of worthy and lawful men of your county, by whom the truth of the matter can be better known), you diligently inquire whether or not [*nec ne* below] there would be any hurt or prejudice, of us or of any others, if we were to grant to ... that he might be able to give and assign three acres and a half of land, and one rood of meadow, with the appurtenances, in ..., to our beloved in Christ the Prior and Convent of ...

habendum et tenendum eisdem magistro et fratribus et successoribus suis imperpetuum in escambium pro duabus acris terre et dimidia et quinque solidatis et sex denaratis redditus cum pertinentiis in eadem villa predicto ... per ipsos magistrum et fratres in feodo dandis et concedendis nec ne

to have and to hold to the same master and friars and their successors for ever, in exchange for two acres and a half of land and five shillings and six pence worth of rent, with the appurtenances, in the same town, to be given and granted in fee to the aforesaid ... by the same master and friars.

Et si sit ad dampnum vel preiudicium nostrum aut aliorum tunc ad quod dampnum et quod preiudicium et quorum et qualiter et quo modo

And if it would be to any hurt or prejudice of us or of any others, then what that hurt or prejudice might be, and of whom, and in what manner and in what way,

et de quo vel de quibus predicta terra et pratum teneantur et per que servicia

and from whom the aforesaid land and meadow are held, and by what service,

et quantum valeant per annum in omnibus exitibus

and how much they are worth annually in all issues,

et qui et quot sunt medii inter nos et prefatum ... de tribus acris terre et dimidia et una roda prati predictis

and who and how many are the mesne tenants between ourselves and the aforenamed ... as regards the aforesaid three acres and a half of land and one rood of meadow.

Et inquisicionem inde distincte et aperte factam nobis sub sigillo tuo et sigillis eorum per quos facta fuerit sine dilacione mittas et hoc breve

And the inquisition thereof, clearly and openly made, you should send to us without delay, under your seal and the seals of those by whom it has been made, with this writ.

Teste me ipso apud … … die … anno regni nostri …
Witnessed by me myself at … on the … day of … in the … year of our reign.

Another situation in which the crown would want to instigate an inquiry was the death of a crown tenant. The crown would want to know who the next heir was, not least because of the possibility of a lucrative wardship if he was under age. An Inquisition Post Mortem would be needed. A writ of *de diem clausit extremum*, "as he has closed his last day," might be issued:

Writ of De Diem Clausit Extremum

… dei gratia Anglie Scotie Francie et Hibernie Rex fidei defensor etc Escaetori suo in comitatu … salutem

… by the grace of God, of England, Scotland, France and Ireland, King, defender of the faith etc, sends greetings to his Escheator in the county of …

Quia … generosus qui de nobis tenuit in capite diem clausit extremum ut accepimur/accepimus

Whereas … gentleman, who held of us in chief, has, we understand, died ["breathed his last" would retain the flavour of "closed the last day"],

Tibi/Vobis precipimus/mandamus quod omnia terras et tenementa de quibus idem … fuit seisitus in dominico suo ut de feodo in balliva tua/vestra die quo obiit sine dilacione capias/capiatis in manum nostram et ea salve custodiri facias/faciatis donec aliud inde preceperimus

We order that you take into our hands without delay all the lands and tenements of which the same … was seised in his demesne as of fee in your Bailiwick on the day that he died, and that you cause them to be safely kept until we have commanded you otherwise in respect thereof,

et per sacramentum proborum et legalium hominum de eadem Balliva tua/vestra per quos rei veritas melius sciri poterit diligenter inquiras

and that (by the oath of worthy and lawful men of your same bailiwick by whom the truth of the matter can be better known) you diligently inquire

quantum terrarum et tenementorum idem/predictus … tenuit de nobis in capite tam in dominico quam in servicio in dicta balliva tua/vestra dicto die quo obiit et quantum de aliis

how much/many lands and tenements the same/aforesaid … held of us in chief, both in demesne and in service, in your said bailiwick, on the day on which he died, and how much of others,

et per quod servicium et quantum terre et tenementa illa valeant per annum in omnibus exitibus

and by what service, and how much those lands and tenements are worth yearly in all issues,

et quo die idem … obiit et quis propinquior heres eius sit et cuius etatis

and on what day the same … died, and who is his next heir, and of what age.

Et inquisicionem inde distincte et aperte factam nobis in Cancellariam nostram / Scaccarium nostrum sub sigillo tuo/vestro et sigillis eorum per quos facta fuerit sine dilacione mittas/mittatis et hoc breve

And the inquisition thereof, distinctly and plainly made, you should send to us in our Chancery/Exchequer without delay, under your seal and the seals of those by whom it has been made, with this writ.

Teste me ipso apud Westmonasterium ... die ... anno regni regis nostri ...
Witnessed by me myself at Westminster on the ... day of ... in the ... year of our reign.

An alternative to a writ of *de diem clausit extremum* to initiate an Inquisition Post Mortem was a writ of *mandamus* [we order]:

Writ of Mandamus

> *... dei gratia Anglie Scotie Francie et Hibernie Rex fidei defensor etc Escaetori suo in Comitatu ... Salutem*
> ..., by the grace of God, of England, Scotland, France and Ireland, King, defender of the faith etc, sends greetings to his Escheator in the County of ...
> *Precipimus tibi quod per sacramentum proborum et legalium hominum de balliva tua per quos rei veritas melius sciri poterit diligenter inquiras quantum terrarum et tenementorum ... generosus defunctus tenuit de nobis in capite tam in dominico quam in servicio in eadem balliva tua die quo obiit et quantum de aliis et per quod servicium et quantum terre et tenementa illa valeant per annum in omnibus exitibus*
> We order you that (by the oath of worthy and lawful men of your Bailiwick, by whom the truth of the matter can be better known) you should diligently inquire how much land and tenements ... gentleman deceased, held of us in chief, both in demesne and in service, in your same bailiwick, and how much of others, on the day on which he died, and by what service, and how much those lands and tenements are worth yearly in all issues,
> *Et quo die idem ... obiit et quis propinquior heres eius sit et cuius etatis et quis vel qui terras et tenementa illa a tempore mortis predicti ... occupavit vel occupaverunt ac exitus et proficua inde percepit vel perceperunt quo titulo qualiter et quomodo*
> And on what day the same ... died, and who is his next heir, and of what age, and what person or persons has or have occupied those lands and tenements since the time of the death of the aforesaid ... and has or have taken the issues and profits thereof, and by what title; how and in what manner?
> *Et inquisicionem inde distincte et aperte factam nobis in cancellariam nostram sub sigillo tuo et sigillis eorum per quos facta fuerit sine dilacione mittas et hoc breve*
> And the inquisition thereof, clearly and openly made, you should send to us in our chancery without delay, under your seal and the seals of those by whom it will have been made, with this writ.
> *Teste meipso apud Westmonasterium ... die ... anno regni nostri ...*
> Witnessed by me myself at Westminster on the ... day of ...in the ... year of our reign.

During the Commonwealth writs were issued in the name of the Keepers of the Liberty of England rather than the monarch, as follows;

> *Custodes libertatis Anglie authoritate Parliamenti ... et ... generosis salutem*
> The keepers of the liberty of England, by authority of Parliament, send greeting to ... and ... gentlemen.

INQUISITION POST MORTEM

Nowadays we understand an *inquisition post mortem* to be an inquiry into the cause of someone's death. The medieval version also followed a death, but its purpose was to protect the Crown's interests when a tenant-in-chief (one holding land directly from the monarch) died. It enabled the authorities to keep track of who held what by recording the land holdings and the name, age and relationship of the person inheriting. If there was no-one to inherit, or if the heir was under age, the crown would claim the land as an escheat or wardship respectively.

On learning of a tenant's death the Chancery would send a writ or commission to the escheator or feodaries of the county involved, ordering them to make enquiries by taking evidence from a jury of local worthies and other landowners. Where the deceased had lands in more than one county there was a separate inquiry in each. If the deceased was a city dweller the writ might go to the mayor. If you don't immediately recognise what kind of writ initiated the inquiry the report of the inquisition will tell you. Sometimes there was no writ because the escheator held an inquiry on his own initiative.

The usual format is to list the deceased's land holdings in order, then to name all the superior lords in order, then to list all the annual values in order. Occasionally, however, all the information about one land holding is given before moving on to the next one. The first format is the easier to work with, because the same land is described three times, giving you more chances to decipher awkward words.

There may be a note in the top centre;

Liberata fuit curie ... die ... Anno ... Regis ... per manus ... generosi escaetoris
This was delivered into court on the ... day of ... in the ... year of the reign of ... by the hands of ..., gentleman, escheator.

The name of the county may be written in the top left hand corner. Then comes the report of the inquiry.

Inquisicio indentata capta apud ... in comitatu ... predicto
Indented inquisition, taken at ... in the county of ... aforesaid
... die ... anno regni domini/domine nostre/nostri ... dei gracia Anglie Francie et Hibernie Regis/Regine fidei defensoris etc ...
on the ... day of ... in the ... year of the reign of our Lord/Lady ..., by the grace of God, of England, France and Ireland, King/Queen, defender of the faith etc,
coram ... armigero/generoso/milite Escaetore dicti/dicte domini/domine Regis/Regine in comitatu predicto
before ... esquire/gentleman/knight, Escheator of our said Lord/Lady the King/Queen in the county aforesaid,
virtute officii sui
by virtue of his office
virtute brevis dicti domini/domine Regis/Regine de

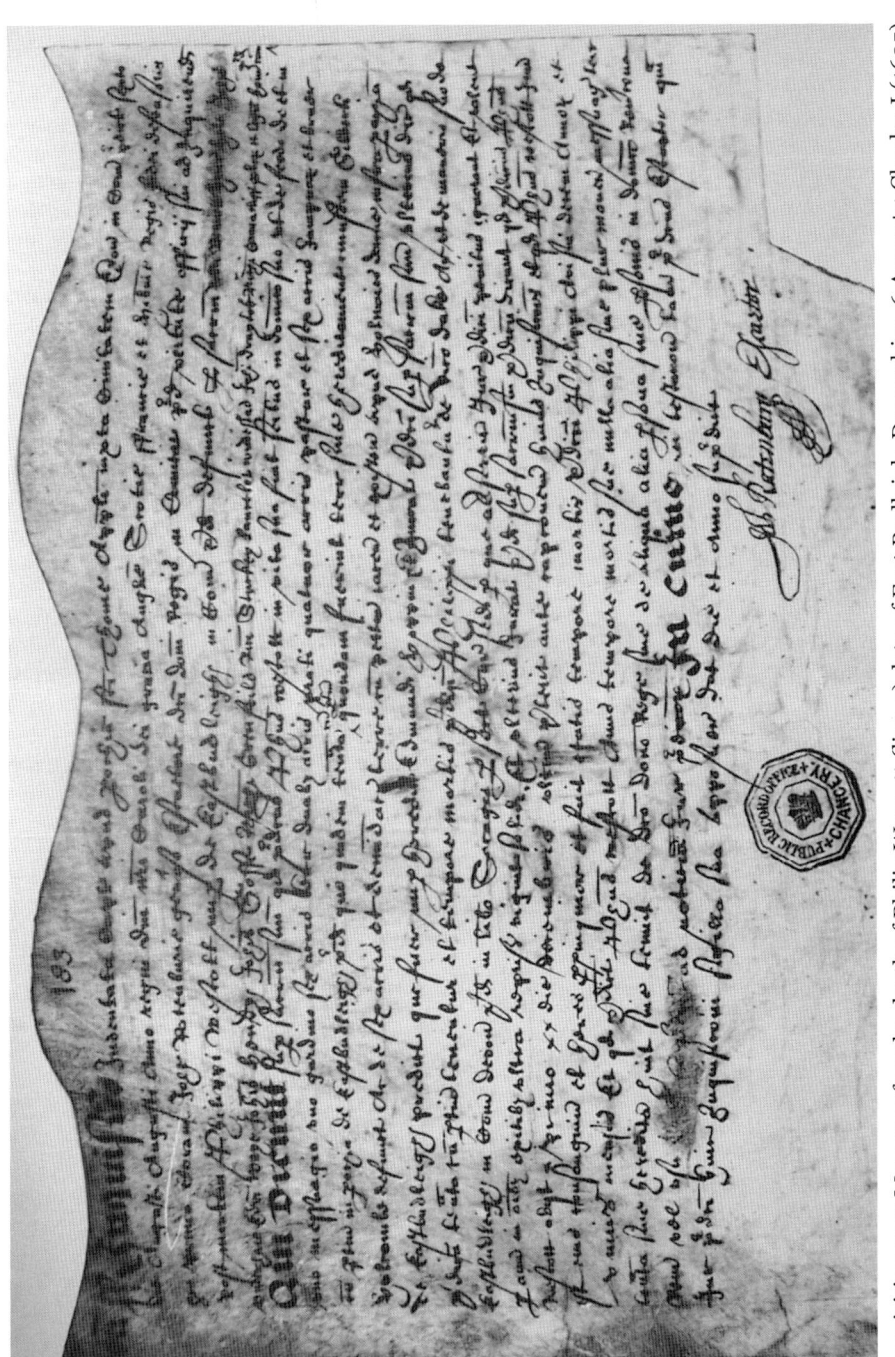

Inquisition post Mortem after the death of Philip Wescott (line 4), late of East Budleigh, Devonshire, 6 August 1 Charles I (1625). From The National Archives, reference C142/687. The word Augusti is repeated in error (line 2).

by virtue of a writ of our said Lord/Lady the King/Queen of [name of writ then given;]
diem clausit extremum [literally, "he closed his last day"]
mandamus [literally, "we order"]
eidem Escaetori directi et huic inquisicioni annexi/consuti
directed to the same Escheator and annexed/sewn to this inquisition,
ad inquirendum post mortem ... nuper de ... in comitatu predicto generosi defuncti
to inquire, following the death of ... late of ... in the county aforesaid, gentleman, deceased,
per sacramentum ......
by the corporal oath of ... ... [the jurors are now listed]
proborum et legalium hominum comitatus predicti
upright and law-abiding men of the county aforesaid
Qui dicunt super sacramentum suum quod predictus ... in dicto brevi nominatus
Who say, upon their corporal oath, that the aforesaid ... named in the said writ [*brevi* not *breve* as it declines like the adjective "brief"]
diu ante obitum suum
a long time before his death
in vita sua et tempore mortis sue
in his lifetime and at the time of his death
die obitus sui
on the day of his death
seisitus fuit in dominico suo ut de feodo
was seised, in his demesne, as of fee
de et in uno mesuagio sive tenemento duobus pomariis et duabus acris pasture cum pertinentiis
of and in one messuage or tenement, two orchards and two acres of pasture, with the appurtenances,
iacentibus scituatis et existentibus in ... in comitatu predicto
lying, situated and being in ... in the county aforesaid,

Previous transactions concerning the land may be recited;

Et sic inde seisitus existens per cartam suam de data ...
And being thus seised thereof, by his deed, of date ...
juratoribus predictis in evidencia ostensam
shown in evidence to the aforesaid jurors
super capcionem huius inquisicionis
upon the taking of this inquisition
dedit concessit et confirmavit omnia etc quibusdam ... et ...
he gave, granted and confirmed all etc to a certain ... and ...
virtute cuius indenture / quorum doni et concessionis ac confirmacionis
by virtue of which indenture / gift and grant and confirmation
ac vigore cuiusdam actus parliamenti in parliamento domini Henrici octavi nuper Regis Anglie tenti apud Westmonasterium in comitatu Middlesexie quarto die Februarii anno regni sui vicesimo septimo de usibus in possessionem transferendis tunc inde editi et provisi

and by force of a certain Act of Parliament, then enacted and provided in respect thereof in the parliament of our lord Henry the Eighth, late King of England, held at Westminster in the county of Middlesex on the fourth day of February in the twenty seventh year of his reign, concerning uses to be transferred into possession

The statute referred to here is the Statute of Uses, 1536/7. The background to it was that the government had become worried by the tendency of landowners to put their land into trust. The trustees would hold the land in trust to allow a specified class of beneficiaries to use and occupy it. Splitting the use from the ownership played havoc with administration, especially tax collection. So the Act provided that the trustees would be ignored and the transferor would be treated as holding the land in the same way he might hold a freehold tenement. It did not take long for lawyers to realise that if the trustees transferred their land to a second set of trustees, only the second set would be ignored, and ownership would remain with the first trustees!

idem/iidem ... fuit/fuerunt inde seisitus/seisiti in dominico suo ut de feodo
the same ... was/were seised thereof in his/their demesne, as of fee,
termino vite sue / vitarum suarum
for the term of his life / their lives
scilicet predictus ... in dicto brevi nominatus ut de libero tenemento
that is to say, the aforesaid ... named in the aforesaid writ, [was seised] as of a free tenement
et possessionem suam inde continuaverit usque in diem capcionis huius inquisicionis
and he continued his possession thereof until the day of the taking of this inquisition
sibi et heredibus masculis de corpore suo legitime procreatis seu procreandis
to him and the heirs male of his body lawfully begotten or to be begotten

The date of the subject's death is given;

Et postea idem/predictus ... sic de omnibus et singulis premissis predictis seisitus existens de tali statu suo obiit / diem suam clausit extremum sic inde seisitus apud ...
And afterwards the same/aforesaid ... being thus seised of all and singular the aforesaid premises, died / breathed his last [a modern substitute for "closed his last day"] thus seised thereof, of such his estate, at ...
... die ... ultimo preterito ante capcionem huius inquisicionis ...
on the ... day of ... last past before the taking of this inquisition ...
... die ... anno regni ...
on the ... day of ... in the ... year of the reign [etc]

The subject's wife may be mentioned;

post cuius mortem dicta ... uxor sua in dictum manerium intravit et fuit inde seisita
after whose death the said ... his wife entered into the said manor and was seised thereof
et ... uxor predicti ... ipsum supervixit et adhuc superstes et in plena vita existit
and ... the wife of the aforesaid ... survived him, and still survives, and is in full life

ac est dotabilis de tertia parte omnium et singulorum predictorum premissorum cum pertinentiis secundum cursum legum communium Anglie

and is entitled to dower of the third part of all and singular the aforesaid premises, with the appurtenances, according to the course of the common laws of England

The superior lords of the property are named, with details of the tenure;

Et juratores predicti ulterius dicunt super sacramentum suum predictum quod predictum ... manerium/tenementa et cetera premissa cum pertinentiis in ... tenetur/tenentur et tempore mortis predicti ... tenebatur/tenebantur

And the jurors aforesaid further say, upon their aforesaid corporal oath, that the aforesaid ... manor/tenements and the rest of the premises, with the appurtenances, in ... is/are held, and at the time of the death of the aforesaid ... was/were held,

de dicto/dicta domino/domina Rege/Regina in capite

of our said Lord/Lady the King/Queen, in chief,

ut de manerio/honore/prebendo suo de ... in comitatu ...

as of his/her manor/honour/prebend of ... in the county of

ut de feodo / per servicium militare / per fidelitatem / in libero socagio / in libero burgagio

as of fee / by military service / by fealty / in free socage / in free burgage

per centesimam partem unius feodi militis et per redditum per annum duodecim denariorum et sectam curie pro omnibus serviciis

by the hundredth part of one knight's fee, and by rent of 12d per annum, and suit of court, for all services [or perhaps;]

sed per que servicia / quam partem feodi militis juratores predicti penitus ignorant

but by what services / what part of a knight's fee the jurors aforesaid are utterly ignorant

The annual value of the property is given, possibly with details of the person who has taken the rents since the death;

et valet/valent clare per annum in omnibus exitibus ultra reprisas ... solidos

and it is / they are worth, clear, by the year, in all issues, over and above reprises, ... shillings

sed quis vel qui terras et tenementa illa a tempore mortis sui predicte occupavit vel occupaverunt ac exitus et proficua inde percepit vel perceperunt quo titulo qualiter et quomodo juratores predicti ignorant

but the aforesaid jurors do not know who [*quis vel qui* because it may be one person or more] occupied [ditto *occupavit vel occupaverunt*] those lands and tenements from the time of his aforesaid death and received [ditto] the issues and profits thereof, [or] by what title, how, and in what manner

The heir is named and his age is given;

Et ulterius juratores predicti dicunt super sacramentum suum predictum

And further the jurors aforesaid say, upon their aforesaid corporal oath

quod ... est filius et heres propinquior predicti ... defuncti et fuit tempore mortis ipsius ... etatis ... annorum ... mensium et ... dierum et non amplius

that ... is the son and next heir of the aforesaid ... deceased, and at the time of the death of the same ... was of the age of ... years ... months and ... days and no more

There is then a statement to the effect that the deceased had no other lands in that county. If you are lucky it will be quite straightforward;

> *Et vero dicunt quod predictus ... non habuit neque tenuit aliqua alia sive plura terra sive tenementa in comitatu predicto*
> And indeed they say that the aforesaid ... did not have or hold any other or further lands or tenements in the county aforesaid.

But it can be very tortuous;

> *Et postremo / ulterius / denique juratores predicti dicunt super sacramentum suum predictum*
> And moreover / further / finally the jurors aforesaid, upon their corporal oath aforesaid, say
> *quod predictus ... defunctus in brevi predicto nominatus*
> that the aforesaid ... deceased, named in the aforesaid writ
> *nec aliquis alius sive aliqui alii ad eius usum*
> nor any other or any others to his use
> *die obitus sui / die quo obiit / tempore mortis sue*
> on the day of his death / on the day on which he died / at the time of his death
> *habuit vel tenuit aut habuerunt vel tenuerunt*
> had or held
> *nulla alia sive plura maneria mesuagia terras tenementa et hereditamenta in dominico possessione servicio usu revercione seu remanere*
> no other or further manors, messuages, lands, tenements and hereditaments, in demesne, possession, service, use, reversion or remainder,
> *de dicto/dicta domino/domina nostro/nostra Rege/Regina*
> of our said Lord/Lady the King/Queen
> *nec de aliquo alio sive de aliquibus aliis*
> nor of any other person or any other persons
> *in dicto comitatu aut alibi ad eorum noticiam / noticiam juratorum predictorum*
> in the said county or elsewhere, to the their notice / the notice of the aforesaid jurors

The witnessing clause is as follows;

> *In cuius rei testimonium uni parti huius inquisicionis indentate penes prefatum Escaetorem remanenti tam prefatus Escaetor quam predicti juratores sigilla sua apposuerunt*
> In witness whereof to one part of this indented inquisition, remaining in the possession of the aforenamed Escheator, both the aforenamed Escheator and the aforesaid Jurors have affixed their seals,
> *alteri vero parti huius/eiusdem inquisicionis penes prefatos juratores predictos remanenti prefatus Escaetor sigillum suum apposuit*
> and indeed to the other part of this / the same inquisition, remaining in the possession of the Jurors aforenamed, the aforenamed Escheator has affixed his seal.

Or more simply;

In cuius rei testimonium huic presenti inquisicioni tam escaetor predictus quam juratores predicti sigilla sua alternatim apposuerunt
In witness whereof to this present inquisition both the aforesaid escheator and the aforesaid jurors have alternately affixed their seals.

Data die anno et loco primo supradictis
Given on the day and year, and in the place, first abovesaid.

There may be a marginal note similar to this;

Transcripta/e inde mittitur/mittuntur in curia/curiis Wardorum et Scacarii per W Ravenscroft
A transcript/s thereof is/are sent into the court/s of Wards and the Exchequer by W Ravenscroft

This is a convenient place to mention Inquisitions ad quod Dampnum. Their format is very similar to the above, but of course they answer a different set of questions. These are detailed in the writ initiating the inquisition – see preceding chapter.

LAND DEEDS

Although we tend to call all documents concerning land and property "deeds", this term should strictly be confined to those executed unilaterally, for example a Deed Poll or a Deed of Gift. Transactions involving two or more parties were dealt with by means of an indenture.

A simple grant of land may begin with a short greeting and an instruction to future readers in the form of a jussive subjunctive; *Sciant omnes* "Let all men know", or *Sciatis* "Know ye". Alternatively a future perfect, *Noveritis* "You shall have known", may be employed. Then there may be an "accusative plus infinitive" construction; "Know ye me to have given" etc;

> *Omnibus Χριστι fidelibus ad quos hoc presens scriptum pervenerit ... de ... in comitatu ... salutem in domino sempiternam*
> To all Christ's faithful to whom this present writing shall have come ... of ... in the county of ... [sends] eternal greetings in the Lord.
> *Sciatis/Noveritis me prefatum ... pro et in consideracione ... librarum legalis monete Anglie meo per ... de ... in comitatu predicto premanibus solutarum unde fateor me plenarie fore satisfactum et persolutum dictumque ... heredes executores et administratores suos inde esse quietos et omnino exoneratos per presentes*
> Know ye / May you know me, the aforenamed ..., for and in consideration of ... pounds of lawful money of England, paid to me beforehand by ... of ... in the aforesaid county, whereof I acknowledge myself to be fully satisfied and paid, and the said ..., his heirs, executors and administrators to be quit and completely exonerated thereof by these presents,
> *dedisse/concessisse/tradidisse/deliberasse et hoc presenti scripto meo confirmasse prefato ... heredibus et assignatis eius imperpetuum*
> to have given/granted/conveyed/delivered, and by this my present writing confirmed, to the aforenamed ..., his heirs and assigns for ever

Rather than the "accusative plus infinitive" a narrative "that" may be used;

> *Sciant presentes et futuri quod ego ... de ... dedi/concessi/tradidi/deliberavi et hac presenti carta mea / scripto meo confirmavi*
> May/Let present and future [people] know that I, ... of ..., have given/granted/conveyed/delivered, and by this my present charter/writing confirmed,
> *... heredibus et assignatis suis imperpetuum*
> to ..., his heirs and assigns for ever
> *pro quadam summa pecunie quam michi dedit premanibus*
> for a certain sum of money which he gave to me beforehand
> *omnia messuagia terras tenementa et hereditamenta cum pertinentiis suis scituata iacentia et existentia infra parochiam de ... modo in tenura sive occupacione prefati ... aut assignatorum suorum*

all the messuages, lands, tenements and hereditaments, with their appurtenances, situated, lying and being within the parish of ... now in the tenure or occupation of the aforenamed ... or his assigns
que nuper habui de dono et feoffamento ...
which I lately had of the gift and feoffment [of] ...

Habendum et tenendum omnia predicta messuagia terras tenementa et hereditamenta cum eorum pertinentiis universis
To have and to hold all the aforesaid messuages, lands, tenements and hereditaments, with all their appurtenances,
prefato ... heredibus et assignatis suis ad solum et unicum opus usum et proficium eiusdem ... heredum et assignatorum suorum imperpetuum
to the aforenamed ..., his heirs and assigns, to the sole and only benefit [this is *opus* "need", not *opus* "work", but "benefit" seems the best compromise], use [or you might prefer to translate *opus usum* as "use, behoof", on the grounds that if "benefit" had been intended, the word *beneficium* could have been used] and profit of the same ..., his heirs and assigns for ever,
libere quiete bene et in pace in feodo et hereditate imperpetuum
freely, quietly, well and in peace in fee and heredity for ever

The following clause was adopted after the statute of *Quia Emptores* in 1290 and can thus be useful for estimating the age of undated documents;

de capitali/capitalibus domino/dominis feodi/feodorum illius/illorum per redditus et servicia inde prius debita et de iure consueta
of the chief lord/s of that/those fee/fees, by the rents and services formerly due in respect thereof and by right accustomed

There may be a clause of warranty;

Et ego/nos vero prefatus/prefati ... ac heredes mei/nostri omnia/tota predicta messuagium ac alia/cetera premissa predicta superius concessa cum omnibus eorum pertinentiis prefato ... heredibus et assignatis suis contra omnes gentes warantizabo/warantizabimus acquietabo/ acquietabimus et imperpetuum defendam/defendemus per presentes
And indeed I/we, the aforenamed ... and my/our heirs will by these presents warrant, acquit and defend all/the whole of the aforesaid messuage and other/the rest of the aforesaid premises above granted, with all their appurtenances, to the aforenamed ..., his heirs and assigns, against all people, for ever.

And witnessing and dating clauses;

In cuius rei testimonium huic presenti scripto meo/nostro sigillum/sigilla meum/nostra apposui/apposuimus
In witness whereof [literally, "in witness of which matter"] I/we have affixed my/our seal/seals to this my/our present writing.

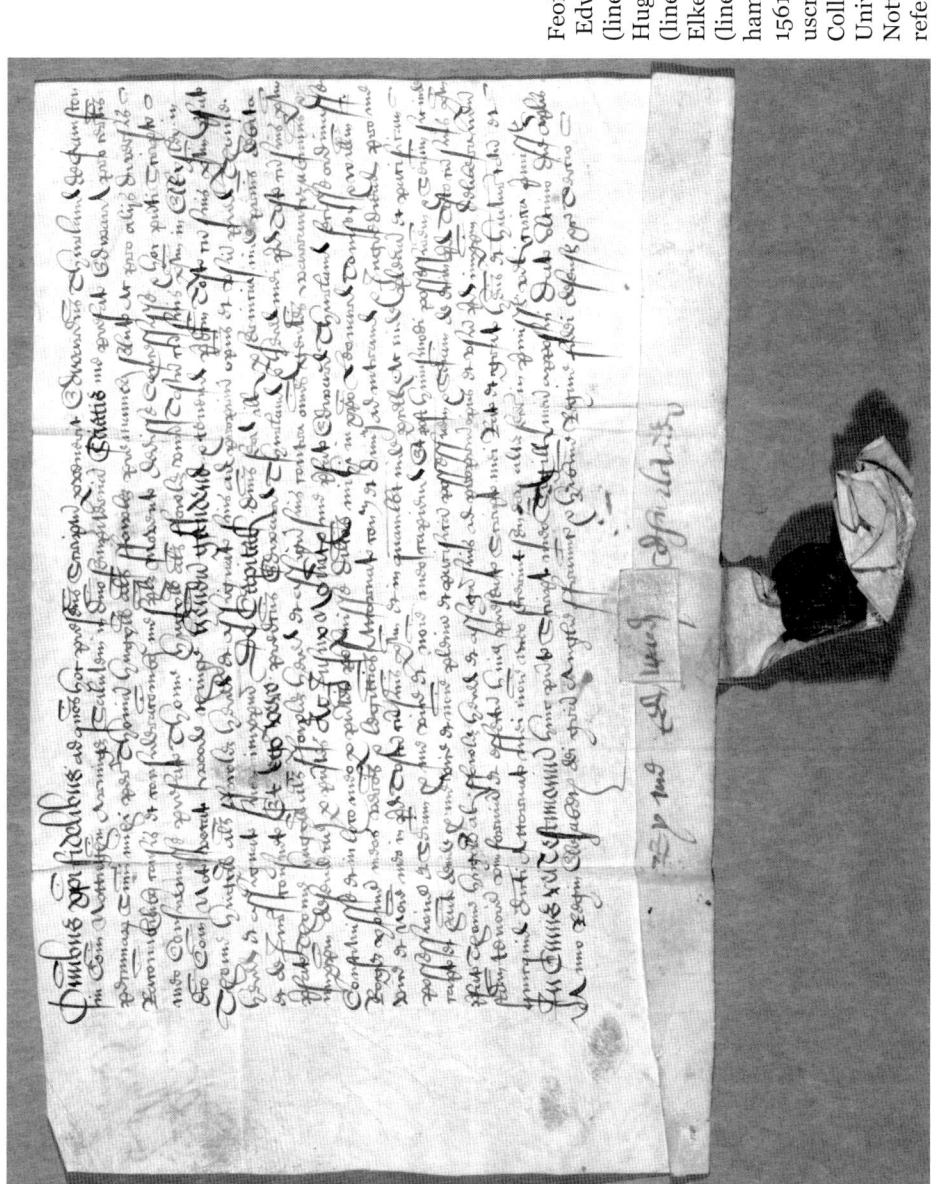

Feoffment from Edward Thurland (line 1) to Thomas Hugyll alias Fowler (line 3) of a toft in Elkesley (Elkysley) (line 5), Nottinghamshire, 30 April 1561. From the Manuscripts and Special Collections of the University of Nottingham, reference Ne D 1383.

Hiis testibus ... ...
These being witnesses ... [their names follow, in the ablative case as this is an "ablative absolute"]
Datum ... die ... anno regni ...domini/domine ... dei gratia Anglie Francie et Hibernie regis/regine fidei defensoris etc ...
Given on the ... day of ... in the ... year of the reign of our Lord/Lady ..., by the grace of God, of England, France and Ireland, King/Queen, defender of the faith etc, ...

The grantor may appoint someone else to deliver seisin, that is to say, to meet the grantee on the premises and hand over a clump of grass or a piece of turf to symbolise the transfer of ownership. In this case the grant may include the following, or a separate document appointing an attorney (a "Power of Attorney") may be prepared.

Noverint universi per presentes me ... de ... in comitatu ...
May all men know, by these presents, that I, ... of ... in the county of ...
Fecisse ordinasse constituisse et loco meo posuisse dilectum michi in christo/χριστο ... meum verum et legitimum attornatum
Have made [literally "know me to have made" etc], ordained, constituted and put in my place my beloved in Christ ... my true and lawful attorney
ad deliberandum pro me et nomine meo ... civi et grocero London aut eius attornato
to deliver, for me and in my name, to ..., Citizen and Grocer of London, or his attorney,
ad intrandum pro me vice et in nomine meo in predicta premissa
to enter into the aforesaid premises, for me, in my place and in my name,
ad plenam ac pacificam possessionem et seisinam inde pro me vice et in nomine meo capiendum
to take full and peaceful possession and seisin thereof for me, in my place and in my name
Et post huiusmodi possessionem et seisinam sic inde captas et habitas ad plenam et pacificam possessionem et seisinam inde pro me vice et in nomine meo prefato ... secundum vim formam et effectum huius presentis carte mee deliberandum
And after this possession and seisin thereof be thus taken and had, to deliver full and peaceful possession and seisin thereof for me, in my place and in my name, to the aforenamed ... according to the force, form and effect of this my present deed
Ratum habeam et gratum totum et quicquid dictus attornatus meus nomine meo fecerit in premissis
And I hold [this reads better than "have"] [as] valid and settled all and everything which my said attorney shall do in my name in the premises. [The subjunctive mood *habeam* rather than the active *habeo* underlines the desire to comply with the undertaking.]
In cuius rei testimonium presentibus sigillum meum apposui
In witness whereof I have affixed my seal to these presents.
Data ... die mensis ... anno regni Regis Edwardi quarti post conquestum primo
Given on the ... day of the month of ... in the first year of the reign of the fourth King Edward after the conquest.

Similarly the grantee may appoint someone else to receive seisin.

Sciatis insuper / Noverint universi per presentes nos prefatos …
May you / all men know, moreover, by these presents, that we, the aforenamed … have [or "know us to have", as before]
attornasse deputasse fecisse ordinasse constituisse et in loco nostro / locis nostris per presentes posuisse dilectos nobis in christo/χριστο … et … nostros veros et legitimos attornatos coniunctim et divisim
attorned, deputed, made, ordained, constituted and by these presents put in our place/s, our beloved in Christ [literally "beloved to us"] … and … our true and lawful attorneys, jointly and severally
ad intrandum pro nobis vice et nominibus nostris de et in omnia premissa superius concessa cum omnibus eorum pertinentiis
to enter, for us and in our place and names, on and into all the premises above granted, with all their appurtenances
ad recipiendum seisinam nomine meo et … uxoris mee et omnium nostrorum suprascriptorum
to receive seisin, in my name and in that of … my wife, and that of all of us abovewritten
ac possessionem et seisinam inde capiendum
and to take possession and seisin thereof
Rata et grata habentes et habituros tota et quicquid dicti attornati nostri nominibus nostris fecerint aut unus eorum fecerit in premissis per presentes
[*habentes et habituros* is difficult to translate directly into English due to the lack of a future participle, but the gist is that the grantors do and will have (a commitment).]
Holding as valid and stable, by these presents, now and in future, all and anything which our said attorneys, or one of them, shall do in the premises in our names.

To make the grantee's title as watertight as possible the grantor might provide a quitclaim. This may be incorporated in the deed of gift/lease, or may be a separate document. The relevant clauses will be similar to the following;

Noveritis / Sciatis universis me prefatum …
May you /all men know that I, the aforenamed …
tam pro quadam competenti pecunie summa mihi premanibus per … de … in comitatu … generosum bene et fideliter persoluta
both for a certain competent sum of money well and faithfully paid to me beforehand by … of … in the county of …, gentleman,
unde fateor me plene fore satisfactum et predictum … et heredes executores et administratores suos inde fore exoneratos et acquietatos per presentes
whereof I acknowledge myself to be fully satisfied, and the aforesaid … and his heirs, executors and administrators to be exonerated and acquitted thereof by these presents,
quam pro diversis aliis bonis causis et consideracionibus me ad hoc specialiter moventibus
and for diverse other good causes and considerations me thereunto especially moving,
concessisse remisisse relaxasse dimisisse et omnino pro/de me et heredibus meis per presentes imperpetuum qietumclamasse prefato …

have granted, remised, released, demised, and utterly and for ever, by these presents, quitclaimed, for/from me and my heirs, to the aforenamed ...

in sua plena possessione et seisina existenti
he being in his full and peaceful possession and seisin,
et heredibus et assignatis suis
and to his heirs and assigns
ad solum opus et usum ipsius ... heredum et assignatorum imperpetuum
to the sole use and benefit [need and use? - see above] of the same ..., his heirs and assigns, for ever,
totum ius statum titulum clameum usum revercionem interesse remanere et demaundum mea quecumque que ego predictus ... unquam habui habeo seu quovismodo in futuro habere potero aut quovismodo heredes mei habere poterint
all my right, estate, title, claim, use, reversion, interest, remainder and demand whatsoever which I, the aforesaid ... ever had, have, or in any way in the future may be able to have, or my heirs in any way whatsoever may be able to have
de et in toto illo mesuagio sive tenemento vocato ... continenti per estimacionem ... acras
of and in all that messuage or tenement called ... containing by estimation ... acres
prefato ... heredibus et assignatis suis
to the aforesaid ... his heirs and assigns
ad proprium opus et usum ipsius ... heredum et assignatorum suorum imperpetuum
to the proper use and benefit of the same ... his heirs and assigns for ever
ita videlicet quod nec ego prefatus ... nec heredes mei nec aliquis alius per me seu nomine meo
so, that is to say, that neither I, the aforenamed ..., nor my heirs, nor any other person through me or in my name,
in futuro / de cetero exigere clamare vel vindicare potero / poterimus
may be able in the future to exact [sometimes translated as "demand"; but then how do you translate *demaundum* below?], claim or appropriate / lay claim to [*vindicare*, sometimes written as *vendicare*]
aut heredes mei exigere clamare vel vindicare poterint
nor may my heirs be able to exact, claim or appropriate / lay claim to
aliquod ius titulum clameum usum statum interesse revercionem remanere vel demaundum quecumque
any right, title, claim, use, estate, interest, reversion, remainder or demand whatsoever
de et in premissis seu de in aliqua parte vel ad aliquam partem seu parcellam eorundem
of and in the premises or in any part thereof, or to any part or parcel of the same
nec debemus quovismodo in futuro
nor ought we to in any way in the future
sed/set ab omni accione iuris iure et calumpnia inde statu titulo clameo interesse et demaundo quibuscumque de cetero in eisdem amoti simus et penitus exclusi imperpetuum per presentes
but may by these presents be for ever removed and utterly excluded from all action of law, right and challenge in respect thereof, estate, title, claim, interest and demand whatsoever in the same in the future
Necnon sciatis/noveritis insuper me prefatum ... pro causis et consideracionibus predictis ulterius remisisse relaxasse et omnino pro me et heredibus executoribus

> *et administratoribus meis imperpetuum quietum clamasse per presentes dicto ... heredibus executoribus et administratoribus suis omnes et omnimodas actiones tam reales quam personales sectas querelas debita compota transgressiones detentiones demanda brevia et brevia de errore ac causas et causas erroris*
> And indeed may you know moreover that I, the aforenamed ... for the causes and considerations aforesaid, have further remised, released, and utterly and for ever, for me and my heirs, executors and administrators, by these presents, quitclaimed, for me, my heirs, executors and administrators, to the said ..., his heirs, executors and administrators, all and all manner of actions, both real and personal, suits, complaints, debts, accounts, trespasses, detinues and demands, writs and writs of error, and causes and causes of error,
> *tangentes vel concernentes aliquam rem vel res modo vel nuper pendentes in aliqua curia sive aliquibus curiis domini Regis nunc de recordo inter partes predictas ac omnes sectas querelas debita compota transgressiones detentiones et demanda quecumque*
> touching or concerning any matter or matters now or lately pending in any of our Lord the now King's court or courts of record [a court of record is one in which a written record of the proceedings is kept] between the parties aforesaid, and all suits, complaints, debts, accounts, trespasses, detinues and demands whatsoever
> *que vel quas versus ipsum ... unquam habui habeo seu quovismodo in futuro habere potero pro messuagiis predictis sive aliqua inde parcella quocumque modo ab origine mundi usque in diem confectionis / usque die date presentium*
> which I ever had against the same ..., or do have, or which I might in any way in the future be able to have, for the messuages aforesaid, or for any parcel thereof, in any way whatsoever, from the beginning of the world up to the day of making / until the day of the date of these presents.

Indentures are described as tripartite, quadripartite and so on to indicate the number of parties to the transaction. How can you tell whether a document is an indenture? Because it's got teeth. It's one half of a pair of indentures. The document was written out twice on the same sheet of parchment, then rolled up and cut across the middle diagonally or in an "S" shape. Each part would end up with a distinctive wavy or jagged top or bottom edge. If there was a subsequent dispute as to whether one of the parts was genuine, the halves could be matched up. Or could not be matched up, if someone had concocted one fraudulently.

How can you tell whether a document is a sale or a lease? Look at the *habendum* clause; in English, "to have and to hold". In a lease it will specify the term for which the recipient is going to hold the land. It may also include the word "demise". In the case of an outright gift or sale it will say "for ever", or in Latin, *imperpetuum*. This is a typical indenture of lease;

> *Hec indentura facta apud ... die Jovis proxima ante festum Apostolorum Simonis et Jude anno regni regis ... post conquestum ...*
> This indenture, made at ... on the Thursday next before the feast of the Apostles Simon and Jude in the ... year of the reign of King ... after the conquest

inter ... ex parte una et ... et ... ex parte altera
between ... on the one part, and ... and ..., on the other part,
testatur quod predictus ... tradidit concessit dimisit ... hac presenti carta indentata confirmavit ...
witnesses [remember, *testor* is a deponent verb; passive in appearance, active in meaning] that the aforesaid ... has handed over, granted, demised, and by this present indented charter has confirmed, to ...,
unum messuagium ... cum suis pertinentiis que ... quondam occupavit
one messuage ... with its appurtenances, which ... formerly occupied,
Habendum et tenendum predictum messuagium cum suis pertinentiis
To have and to hold the aforesaid messuage with its appurtenances
ad terminum sexaginta annorum proxime sequentium post datam presentium et plenarie completorum
for the term [literally "to the end"] of sixty years fully completed next following after the date of these presents [or maybe;]
pro termino vite eorum et unius eorum diutius viventis
for the term of their life and that of the one of them living longest
Reddendum inde annuatim michi et heredibus meis ... usualis monete ad quatuor anni terminos videlicet ad festa Annunciacionis beate Marie Nativitatis Sancti Johannis Baptiste Sancti Michaelis Archangeli et Sancti Andree Apostoli per equales porciones
Yielding annually in respect thereof, to me and my heirs, ... of usual money at four terms of the year, that is to say, at the feasts of the Annunciation of the Blessed Mary, the Nativity of Saint John the Baptist, Saint Michael the Archangel, and Saint Andrew the Apostle, by equal portions.
et dabunt herietum secundum consuetudinem manerii
and they will give heriot according to the custom of the manor.
Et predicti ... manutenebunt et sustentabunt/sustinebunt dictum messuagium cum suis pertinentiis durante vita eorum
And the aforesaid ... will maintain and sustain the said messuage, with its appurtenances, during their life [literally, "the life of them enduring"; ablative absolute],
et in adeo bono statu seu meliori quo illi receperunt dimittent
and will give it back in as good a state as they received it, or better.

A condition in the nature of a mortgage may be included;

Proviso semper quod si predictus ... vel heredes seu assignati sui non solvant seu solvi faciant eidem ... executoribus administratoribus vel assignatis suis summam centum et quindecim librarum legalis monete Anglie temporibus et locis modo et forma prout in indenturis supraspecificatis continetur et exprimitur
Provided always that if the aforesaid ... or his heirs or assigns should not pay or cause to be paid to the same ..., his executors, administrators or assigns, the sum of one hundred and fifteen pounds of lawful money of England at the times and places, and in manner and form, just as is contained and expressed in the above-specified indentures,
quod tunc et deinceps pro defectu talis solucionis hoc presens scriptum indentatum et totum et quicquid in eodem exprimitum seu contentum et omnes et singuli status

> *eidem ... vel heredibus suis vigore seu ratione eiusdem scripti facta seu habita et liberacio seisine premissorum seu alicuius inde parcelle virtute huius presentis scripti fienda seu habenda vacua irritata et nullius vigoris in lege existant et adiudicentur*

> that then and thenceforth, for want of such payment, this present indented writing, and all and anything expressed or contained in the same, and all and singular the estates made or had to the same ... or his heirs by force or reason of the same writing, and the livery of seisin of the premises, or of any parcel thereof, to be made or had by virtue of this present writing, should stand and be adjudged as void, erased, and of no force in law,

> *et quod tunc et deinceps bene licebit eidem ... et heredibus eius in predicta mesuagium terras tenementa et cetera premissa et quamlibet inde parcellam cum singulis suis pertinentiis reintrare ac eadem rehabere et retinere ut in statu suo pristino aliqua re seu materia in presenti scripto contenta seu specificata in contrarium inde non obstanti*

> and that then and thenceforth it shall be well allowed to the same ... and his heirs to re-enter into the aforesaid messuage, lands, tenements and the rest of the premises, and every parcel thereof, with all their appurtenances, and to have and to retain the same again as in their original state, notwithstanding any matter or thing contained or specified to the contrary thereof in the present writing.

There may be clauses of distress. Distraint is the right of a creditor to enter a debtor's property and take belongings to satisfy the debt. The goods removed are known as the distresses.

> *Et si contingat dictum redditum ad aliquem terminum predictum in parte vel in toto aretro fore/esse non solutum pro quadraginta diebus post aliquem terminum predictum tunc bene liceat predicto ... in predicto messuagio cum suis pertinentiis distringere et distringiones/districciones retinere quousque de predicto redditu aretro esse non soluto fuerit eis satisfactum*

> And if it should happen the said rent to be in arrears, unpaid in part or in full, at any term aforesaid, for forty days after any term aforesaid, then it is well licit/lawful/permitted to/for the aforesaid ... to distrain in the aforesaid messuage, with its appurtenances, and to retain the distresses until the aforesaid rent to be in arrears unpaid shall have been satisfied to them

> *Et si distringiones/districciones suficientes inveniri non poterit in messuagio predicto cum suis pertinentiis tunc bene licebit predicto ... in tenementis predictis cum suis pertinentiis reintrare et in prestino statu retinere non obstante donacio predicta*

> And if it is not possible for sufficient distresses to be found in the messuage aforesaid, with its appurtenances, then it shall be well licit/lawful/permitted for the aforesaid ... to re-enter into the tenements aforesaid, with their appurtenances, and to retain them in their pristine state, notwithstanding the gift aforesaid.

There may also be clauses of warranty;

> *Et predictus ... predictum messuagium cum pertinentiis suis predicto ... et assignatis suis termino predicto durante contra omnes gentes warantizabit et defendet*

And the aforesaid ... will warrant and defend the aforesaid messuage, with its appurtenances, to the aforesaid ... and his assigns, against all men, during the term aforesaid.

and the usual dating and witnessing clauses;

In cuius rei testimonium partes predicti sigilla sua alternatim apposuerunt
In witness whereof the parties aforesaid have alternately affixed their seals.
Data apud ... die et Anno Supradictis
Given at ... on the day and year abovesaid.

In 1536 the Statute of Enrolments (or Inrollments as it was spelt in the act) was enacted, saying that all documents conveying land had to be recorded in a public registry. Landowners didn't like the sound of this so their lawyers looked for ways of transferring ownership without an outright conveyance.

One of the most popular methods was the lease and release. This involved two distinct steps, usually done on two consecutive days. First you leased your land to someone, but you retained the freehold interest, so you hadn't disposed of your land. Then you released your interest. The tenant then had the freehold as well, and was left paying rent to himself, so to him this was effectively a purchase.

Just to confuse us, the initial lease was called a bargain and sale. It was all very conventional, the term usually being one year and the rent a one-off payment of 5 shillings. When the release was made the genuine consideration changed hands; this was "the real deal". The two halves have often become separated over the years and if you have just the lease it can be easy to take it at face value.

FINAL CONCORD

For many centuries there was no provision for registering title to land as a matter of course. This meant that people wanting to buy and sell land were in an awkward position, because the purchaser would not want to hand over any cash unless he could be sure of obtaining a legal title to the land.

The King's courts had always been available to settle disputes concerning land. A young orphan might come of age and claim his guardian had not handed over all the lands he was entitled to, or a knight might return from the crusades and find squatters in his castle and local farmers using his land. The courts would make a decision and from then on the winning party could point to the judgment as his legal title.

Medieval lawyers therefore had the bright idea of dressing up sales as legal disputes. X wished to sell his land to Y for £20. X would go to court, usually the Court of Common Pleas, and claim that Y had wrongly entered into occupation of his land. After making the complaint, X would go back to the court and say that he had come to an arrangement with Y to the effect that Y could keep possession on payment of compensation of £20. So the fact that you have a document talking about the King's Court at Westminster, and giving the names of four judges, doesn't necessarily mean there was a dispute.

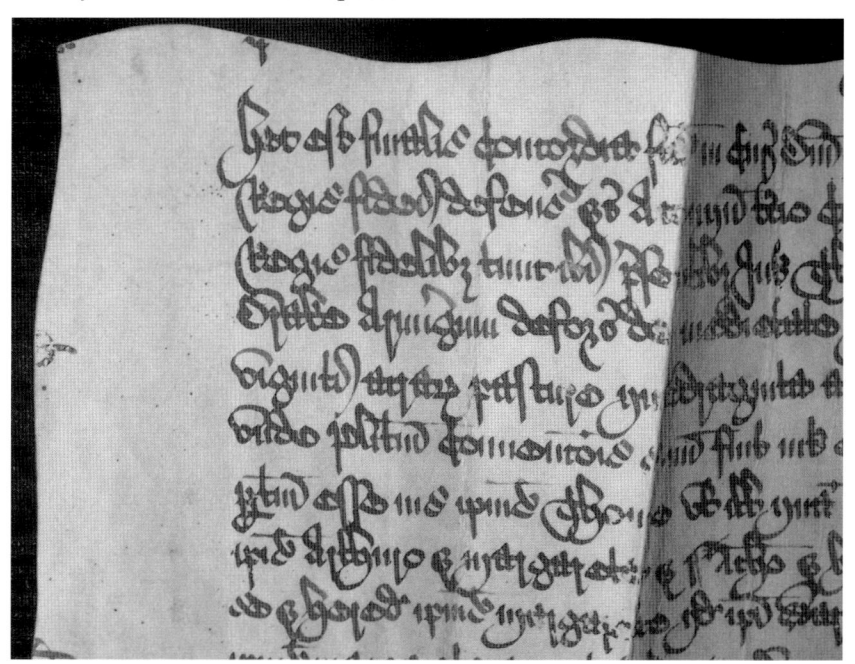

The deforciant's copy of a Fine or Final Concord, showing the two indented edges.

The court would record the agreement as if it were a decision of the court, and this record may be referred to as a Final Concord or as a Foot of Fine.

The first description is taken from the opening words, *Hec est finalis concordia*, "This is the final agreement." The agreement was written out three times; one copy for the plaintiff, one for the defendant, and one for the court. A large sheet of parchment was divided into three sections by means of an imaginary inverted capital letter T. The parchment was then swivelled round 90° to the right, and the plaintiff's and defendant's copies were written in the two sections on the right, one above the other. Next the parchment was put back in its original position and the court's copy was written at the bottom. Finally the copies were separated and given to the respective parties.

The whole agreement was a "fine", not because there was any financial punishment involved, but from the Norman French word *fin*, meaning "end". The agreement brought an end to the matter. The official copy, being the one from the foot of the parchment and preserved in the court records, gave rise to the second description; Foot of Fine.

The sections given to the parties are of course the ones usually held in family archives and estate papers. Sometimes however it is a certified copy of the court record, along the following lines;

Jacobus dei gracia Anglie Scotie Francie et Hibernie Rex fidei defensor etc omnibus ad quos presentes littere nostre pervenerint salutem

James, by the grace of God, of England, Scotland, France and Ireland, King, defender of the faith etc, to all to whom these present letters may come, greeting.

Sciatis quod inter recorda ac pedes finium cum proclamationibus inde factis secundum formam statuti in huiusmodi casu nuper editi provisique coram Justiciariis nostris de Banco apud Westmonasterium

May you know that among the records and feet of fines, with proclamations thereon made according to the form of the statute lately enacted and provided in this case before our Justices of the Bench at Westminster,

Et de termino Sancti Hillarii anno regni nostri regnorum nostrorum Anglie Francie et Hibernie decimo nono et Scotie quinquagesimo quinto

And [in the records] of Hillary Term in the years of our reigns [see below], of England, France and Ireland the nineteenth, and of Scotland the fifty fifth,

Continetur sic
Is contained, thus;

The record proper then follows.

Hec est finalis concordia facta in Curia domini/domine Regis/Regine apud Westmonasterium/Eboracum
This is the final concord, made in the Court of our Lord the King/Queen at Westminster/York
in Crastino/in (s/in quindena
on the day afte   ne octave [eight days following]/in the quindene [fifteen days following]

> *sancti Martini/Hillarii/sancte Trinitatis*
> of Saint Martin/Hillary/Holy Trinity
> *anno regnorum ... dei gracia Magne Britannie / Anglie Scotie Francie et Hibernie Regis/Regine fidei defensoris etc ...*
> in the ... year of the reigns of ... by the grace of God, King/Queen of Great Britain / England, Scotland, France and Ireland, defender of the faith etc,

Sometimes the phrase *a conquestu* "from the conquest" is inserted. "The eighth King Henry from the conquest" might make sense, but "Elizabeth from the conquest" hardly does. Another peculiarity is that it is always *anno regnorum* not *anno regni*. This makes sense where a king and queen are ruling jointly, or the monarch in question has two kingdoms, but why "the reigns of Elizabeth" etc? I have seen it justified as relating to the separate realms of England, Scotland, France and Ireland, but this formula does not occur in other kinds of document.

> *coram ... Justiciariis et aliis domini/domine Regis/Regine fidelibus tunc ibi presentibus*
> before ... Justiciars, and other faithful [subjects] of our Lord/Lady the King/Queen then and there present,
> *inter AA querentes/petentes et BB deforceantes/tenentes*
> between AA, querents/plaintiffs, and BB, deforciants/defendants,
> *de duobus mesuagiis etc etc cum pertinentiis in ...*
> concerning two messuages etc etc, with the appurtenances, in ...
> *unde placitum conventionis summonitum fuit inter eos in eadem/prefata curia videlicet/scilicet*
> in respect whereof a plea of agreement was summoned between them in the same/aforenamed court, that is to say,
> *quod predictus/predicti BB recognovit/recognoverunt tota predicta tenementa cum pertinentiis esse ius ipsius AA*
> that the aforesaid BB has/have recognised all the aforesaid tenements, with the appurtenances, to be the right of the same AA,
> *ut illa que idem/iidem AA habet/habent de dono predicti/predictorum BB*
> as that which the same AA has/have of the gift of the aforesaid BB
> *Et ille/illi remisit/remiserunt et quietaclamavit/quietaclamaverunt de ipsis BB et heredibus suis/ipsius/predicti ... predicto AA et heredibus suis/ipsius/predicti ... imperpetuum*
> And he/they has/have remised and quitclaimed them, from themselves, BB, and his/their heirs / the heirs of the same/aforesaid ... to the aforesaid AA and his/their heirs / the heirs of the same / aforesaid ... for ever
> *Et preterea idem/iidem BB concessit/concesserunt pro se et heredibus suis/ipsius ... quod ipse/ipsi warantizabit/warantizabunt predicto/predictis AA et heredibus suis/ipsius AA predicta tenementa cum pertinentiis contra omnes homines imperpetuum*
> And beyond this the same BB has/have granted, for him/them and his/their/the heirs of the same ..., that he/they will warrant the aforesaid tenements, with their appurtenances, to the aforesaid AA and their/the heirs of the same AA, against all men for ever.

The warranty clause may be repeated with various combinations of plaintiffs and defendants, the extra paragraphs being introduced by *et ulterius* [and further], *et insuper* [and moreover], *et etiam/eciam* [and also].

> *Et pro hac recognicione remissione quietaclamacione warantia fine et concordia idem/iidem AA dedit/dederunt ipsis/predictis BB ... libras sterlingorum / marcas argenti*
> And for this recognizance, remise, quitclaim, warranty, fine and agreement, the same AA has/have given to the same BB ... pounds sterling / marks of silver.

The following clauses may also appear;

> *Habendum et Tenendum eidem AA et heredibus suis*
> To have and to hold to the same AA and his heirs
> *de predicto BB et heredibus suis imperpetuum*
> of the aforesaid BB and his heirs, for ever,
> *de capitalibus dominis feodi illius per servicia que ad predictum mesuagium pertinent imperpetuum*
> of the chief lords of that fee, by the services which pertain to the aforesaid messuage, for ever
> *Reddendo inde annuatim ... solidos ad duos terminos anni videlicet medietatem ad Paschem et alia medietatem ad festum Sancti Michaelis pro omne servicio et exactione*
> Yielding annually in respect thereof ... shillings, at two terms of the year, that is to say, one half at Easter and the other half at the feast of Saint Michael, for all service and exaction.
> *Et sciendum quod predictum AA et eius heredes acquietabunt eandem terram versus capitales dominos feodi illius de serviciis que ad eos inde pertinent*
> And it is to be known that the aforesaid AA and his heirs will acquit the same land against the chief lords of that fee of the services which pertain to them in respect thereof.

You may find the dates of proclamations endorsed on the document, for example;

> *Secundum formam statuti*
> According to the form of the statute
> *Prima proclamacio facta fuit tricesimo die Junii termino sancte Trinitatis Anno tricesimo octavo Regine infrascripte*
> The first proclamation was made on the thirtieth day of June in Trinity term in the thirty eighth year of the within-written queen
> *Secunda proclamacio facta fuit decimo die Novembris termino sancti Michaelis Anno tricesimo octavo Regine infrascripte*
> The second proclamation was made on the tenth day of November in Michaelmas term in the thirty eighth year of the within-written queen

and so on.

RECOVERY OF SEISIN

An alternative to a Foot of Fine was a Common Recovery or Recovery of Seisin. This complicated procedure was called a recovery as it involved the pretence that the purchaser was the genuine owner recovering his land from a fraudster.

The procedure was used where someone was in possession of land, but the land was encumbered by an entail. In other words the possessor (the "tenant in tail") had only a life interest, and after his death the land would descend to some other preordained person or series of people, usually his male heirs. To defeat this intention it was necessary to go through a number of artificial steps involving a friend, agent or lawyer (the "tenant to the praecipe") and even some fictitious characters.

The cast always included Hugh Hunt, often Edward Howse, and sometimes John Doe or Richard Roe; these legal pantomimes (known technically as collusive actions) were played out to a fixed script!

It was all worthwhile, however, because a recovery barred all contingent remainders; that is to say, it broke the entail and caused the land to revert to freehold status. The court judgment is written down in an exemplification which

Hugh Hunt (line 2) and John Wheeler (line 4) make their appearance in a Recovery concerning Raddon, Shobrooke (Showbrooke) and Combe Martin (Coombmarten) (line 1) in Devonshire.

is a fabulous thing to look at, with its monarch's portrait, stylised script, and royal seal.

Let's say I'm Lord Broke, and I'm short of a bob or two. I want to sell some of my inheritance to a youngster who's made a pile in the city. Nothing changes. Let's call him Johnny Cash. Now, I don't want my name dragged through the courts so I convey the land to some stooge, whom we'll call Sam Stooge.

Johnny Cash wants the land so he sues Sam Stooge saying Sam is occupying his land unlawfully. Sam Stooge's defence, not surprisingly, is that he got the land from me. But Johnny Cash says I only possessed it because I got it from Hugh Hunt, and Hugh Hunt had wrongfully disseised Johnny in the first place.

The court calls me to give my account. I'm called the vouchee. I tell a different tale. I say I got it from John Wheeler. The judge then calls John Wheeler. He is called the common vouchee. Now there are two possibilities.

In the first the court usher (to whom I have already spoken, and paid a small fee) says that John Wheeler has had to leave the court and seeks an adjournment. In the other scenario the court crier, or some dubious character whom I have picked up in the street outside but who knows the ropes, turns up, identifies himself as John Wheeler, and asks permission to withdraw and confer with me. Or he may even simply dash out of the courtroom!

Either way the court has to adjourn, but when it reconvenes the usher reports that John Wheeler can't be found. This means that my story can't be corroborated, and judgment is given in favour of Johnny Cash. He "recovers" the land, and what's more he gets it freehold, without any encumbrances.

John Wheeler is found to be in contempt of court. Johnny Cash (the demandant) is allowed to recover the land from Sam Stooge (the tenant to the praecipe). Sam is given the right to claim compensation from John Wheeler (the common vouchee), but he is either non-existent or a "man of straw", so he is placed in the court's mercy (ie made liable to a fine) instead.

As I say, it's all a pantomime. The supporting cast always have the same names. In some circumstances, if the proceedings have been started by means of a writ of entry, the tenant in tail calls John Doe and Richard Roe as sureties. If other people such as trustees or mortgagors have interests in the land, you may see Edward Howse mentioned.

In the following example, TT denotes the Tenant in Tail, TP the Tenant to the Praecipe, D the Demandant, and CV the Common Vouchee.

> ... dei gracia Anglie Francie et Hibernie Rex/Regina fidei defensor etc omnibus ad quos presentes littere nostre pervenerint salutem
> ..., by the grace of God, King/Queen of England, France and Ireland, defender of the faith etc, [sends] greeting to all to whom these our present letters shall have come.
> Sciatis quod inter placita terre irrotulata apud Westmonasterium coram Domino J milite et sociis suis Justiciariis nostris de Banco Regis/Regine et de termino Sancti Hillarii anno regni nostri undecimo rotulo/rotula Cx continetur/irrotulatur sic scilicet/videlicet

Know ye / May you know that amongst the pleas of land enrolled at Westminster before Sir J, knight, and his fellows, our Justices of the King's/Queen's Bench, and [amongst the pleas] of Saint Hillary term in the eleventh year of our reign, in roll 110, it is contained/enrolled thus, that is to say;

[County]

D generosus in propria persona sua / per ... attornatum suum petit versus TP
D, gentleman, in his own person / through ..., his attorney, seeks, against TP,
unum tenementum et quatuor acras pasture cum pertinentiis in ... ut ius et hereditatem suam
one tenement and four acres of pasture, with the appurtenances, in ..., as his right and inheritance,
et in que idem TP non habet ingressum nisi post disseisinam quam Hugo Hunt inde iniuste et sine iudicio fecit prefati D infra triginta annos iam ultimos elapsos etc
and into which the same TP has no right of entry except after the disseisin which Hugh Hunt, unjustly and without judgment, made thereof of the aforenamed D within the thirty years now last past etc

The reference to thirty years always appears. Presumably actions had to be commenced within thirty years of an alleged wrong, otherwise they were "time barred".

Et unde dicit quod ipsemet fuit seisitus de tenemento predicto cum pertinentiis in dominico suo ut de feodo et iure tempore pacis tempore domini Regis/Regine nunc capiendo inde expletas ad valenciam etc Et in que etc Et inde producit sectam etc
And whereupon he says that he himself was seised of the tenement aforesaid, with the appurtenances, in his demesne, as of fee and right, in time of peace, in the time of our Lord the now King/Queen, by taking thereof the issues to the value etc, and into which etc, and thereof he brings suit etc.
et predictus TP in propria persona sua / per attornatum suum venit /alias venit Et defendit ius suum quando etc
and the aforesaid TP, in his own person / through his attorney, comes / came at another time, and defends his right when etc,
et vocat inde ad warantiam TT qui presens est hic in curia / modo per summonitam ei in comitatu predicto factam in propria persona sua per ... attornatum suum venit
and thereupon calls to warrant TT, who is present here in court / now, by summons made to him in the county aforesaid, in his own person / through his attorney, comes
et gratis tenementa predicta cum pertinentiis ei warantizat etc
and freely warrants the aforesaid tenements, with their appurtenances, to him etc.
Et super hoc predictus D petit versus ipsum TT tenentem per warantiam suam tenementa predicta cum pertinentiis in forma predicta etc
And hereupon the aforesaid D seeks, against the same TT, tenant by his own warranty, the aforesaid tenements, with their appurtenances, in the manner aforesaid etc,

et unde dicit quod ipsemet fuit seisitus de tenementis predictis cum pertinentiis in dominico suo ut de feodo et iure tempore pacis tempore domini/domine Regis/Regine nunc capiendo inde expletas ad valenciam etc Et in que etc Et inde producit sectam etc

and whereupon he says that he himself was seised of the tenements aforesaid, with the appurtenances, in his demesne, as of fee and right, in time of peace, in the time of our Lord/Lady the present King/Queen, by taking the issues thereof to the value etc, and into which etc, and thereof he brings his suit etc.

Et predictus TT tenens per warantiam suam defendit ius suum quando etc

And the aforesaid TT, tenant by his own warranty, defends his right when etc,

et ulterius vocat inde ad warantiam CV qui similiter presens est hic in curia in propria persona sua

and further vouches then to warranty CV, who is likewise present here in court in his own person,

et gratis tenementa predicta cum pertinentiis ei warantizat etc

and freely warrants the aforesaid tenements, with their appurtenances, to him etc.

Et super hoc predictus D petit versus ipsum CV tenentem per warantiam suam tenementa predicta cum pertinentiis in forma predicta etc

And upon this the aforesaid D seeks, against the same CV, tenant by his warranty, the aforesaid tenements, with their appurtenances, in the manner aforesaid etc,

et unde dicit quod ipsemet fuit seisitus de tenementis predictis cum pertinentiis in dominico suo ut de feodo et iure tempore pacis tempore domini/domine Regis/Regine nunc capiendo inde expletas ad valentiam etc Et in que etc Et inde producit sectam etc

and whereupon he says that he himself was seised of the tenements aforesaid, with the appurtenances, in his demesne, as of fee and right, in time of peace, in the time of our Lord/Lady the present King/Queen, by taking the issues thereof to the value etc, and into which etc, and thereof he brings his suit etc.

Et predictus CV tenens per warantiam suam defendit ius suum quando etc

And the aforesaid CV, tenant by his warranty, defends his right when etc,

et dicit quod predictus Hugo non disseisivit prefatum D de tenementis predictis cum pertinentiis prout idem D per breve et narrationem suam predictam superius supponit

and says that the aforesaid Hugh did not disseise the aforenamed D of the aforesaid tenements, with their appurtenances, as the same D supposes above by his writ and statement,

et de hoc ponit se super patriam etc

and he puts himself before the court on this point etc.

Et predictus D petit licentiam inde interloquendi et habet etc

And the aforesaid D thereupon seeks leave to imparl, and he has this [granted] etc.

Et postea idem D revenit hic in curiam isto eodem termino in propria persona sua / per attornatum suum predictum

And afterwards the same D comes back here into Court, in the same Term, in his own person /through his attorney aforesaid,

et predictus CV licet solemniter exactus non revenit set in contemptu curie recessit Et defaltum facit

and the aforesaid CV, although solemnly charged, did not come back, but in contempt of court withdrew, and he makes default.

Ideo consideratum est quod predictus D recuperet seisinam suam versus predictum/prefatum TP de tenementis predictis cum pertinentiis
Therefore it is considered that the aforesaid D should recover his seisin, against the aforesaid/aforenamed TP, of the aforesaid tenements, with the appurtenances,
et quod idem TP habeat de terra predicti TT ad valentiam etc
and that the same TP should have, from the land of the aforesaid TT, to the value etc,
et quod idem TT ulterius habeat de terra predicti CV ad valenciam etc
and further that the same TT should have, from the land of the aforesaid CV, to the value etc.
Et idem CV in misericordia etc
And the same CV is amerced [literally "in mercy"] etc.

Et super hoc predictus D petit breve domini/domine Regis/Regine vicecomiti comitatus predicti dirigendum de habere faciendo ei plenariam seisinam de tenementis predictis cum pertinentiis
And hereupon the aforesaid D seeks a writ of our Lord/Lady the King/Queen, to be directed to the Sheriff of the aforesaid County, to cause him to allow him/them to have full seisin of the aforesaid tenements, with the appurtenances,
et ei conceditur retornabile hic in octabis Purificationis beate Marie etc
and it is granted to him/them, returnable here in the octave of the Purification of the blessed Mary etc.

Que omnia et singula ad requisitionem predicti D tenore presentium duximus exemplificanda
All and singular of which, at the request of the same D, we think fit to be exemplified by the tenor of these presents.
In cuius rei testimonium sigillum nostrum ad brevia in banco predicto sigillandum deputatum presentibus apponi fecimus
In witness whereof we have caused to be affixed to these presents our seal appointed for sealing writs in the aforesaid Bench.

Ad quem diem / postea scilicet ... die ... isto eodem termino venit hic in curiam predictus D in propria persona sua / per attornatum suum predictum
On which day / and afterwards, that is to say, on the ... day of ... in this same term, the aforesaid D comes here into court in his own person / through his attorney aforesaid,
et vicecomes videlicet ... modo mandat quod ipse virtute brevis illius/predicti sibi directi ... die ... ultimo preterito habere fecerit prefatis D plenariam seisinam de tenementis predictis cum pertinentiis prout per breve illud sibi preceptum fuit etc
and the Sheriff, that is to say ..., now reports that he, by virtue of that/the aforesaid writ [of deraignment] directed to him on the ... day of ... last past, has caused [*fecerit* not *fecit*; subjunctive because it is reported speech] the aforenamed D to have full seisin of the aforesaid tenements, with the appurtenances, just as he was ordered by that writ etc
Teste ... apud Westmonasterium ... die ... anno regni nostri ...
Witnessed by ... at Westminster on the ... day of ... in the ... year of our reign.

COPYHOLDS AND SURRENDERS

Manor courts had many functions, and many books have been written about them and their records. I am therefore limiting the aspects considered here to copyholds and surrenders.

Copyhold was a method of tenure of land. The evidence of title was the entry in the manor court rolls. The tenant was given a copy of the entry, hence the name. The copyhold could be surrendered, and sometimes a family would arrange a surrender so that the holding passed to the next generation. Often the copyhold was for the lives of three tenants "or the longest living of them", so that it passed automatically on the first two deaths, but it was still customary to add a new name after each death.

A tenant might surrender his copyhold back to the lord "to the purposes of" his will. He would then nominate the next tenant in his will.

The records are court records, and like those from other courts, they can suffer from an inconsistent use of tenses. It is quite possible to see "he took from the lord", "he gives as a fine" and "he made fealty" in the same entry, for example.

Surrender

> *Visus Fraunci Plegii cum Curia Baronis ... ibidem tenta ... die ... Anno Regni Regis ... Magne Britannie etc ...*
> View of Frankpledge with Court Baron [of so-and-so (the lord of the manor)] held in the same place on the ... day of ... in the ... year of the reign of ..., King of Great Britain etc,
> *coram ... generoso senescallo ibidem*
> before ... gentleman, steward in the same place.
> *Ad hanc curiam venerunt / testatum est quod*
> To this court came / at this court it was witnessed that
> *... et ... uxor ejus (predicta ... sola et secreta examinata et confessa per senescallum curie predicte)*
> ... and ... his wife, (the aforesaid ... having been examined and heard, alone and secretly, by the steward of the aforesaid court),
> *et sursumreddiderunt in manus domini et etiam remiserunt relaxaverunt et imperpetuum quietaclamaverunt*
> and surrendered into the hands of the lord, and also remised, released and for ever quitclaimed,
> *per manus ... customarii tenentis predicti manerii*
> through the hands of ..., a customary tenant of the aforesaid manor,
> *per senescallum suum predicti*
> through his aforesaid steward
> *tota eorum jus et titulum de in et ad*
> all their right and title of, in and to
> *unum messuagium in ... nuper ... et prius ... iacens et existens infra manerium de ...*
> one messuage in ... late ... [name of previous tenant given in genitive case] and formerly ... [ditto] lying and being within the manor of ...

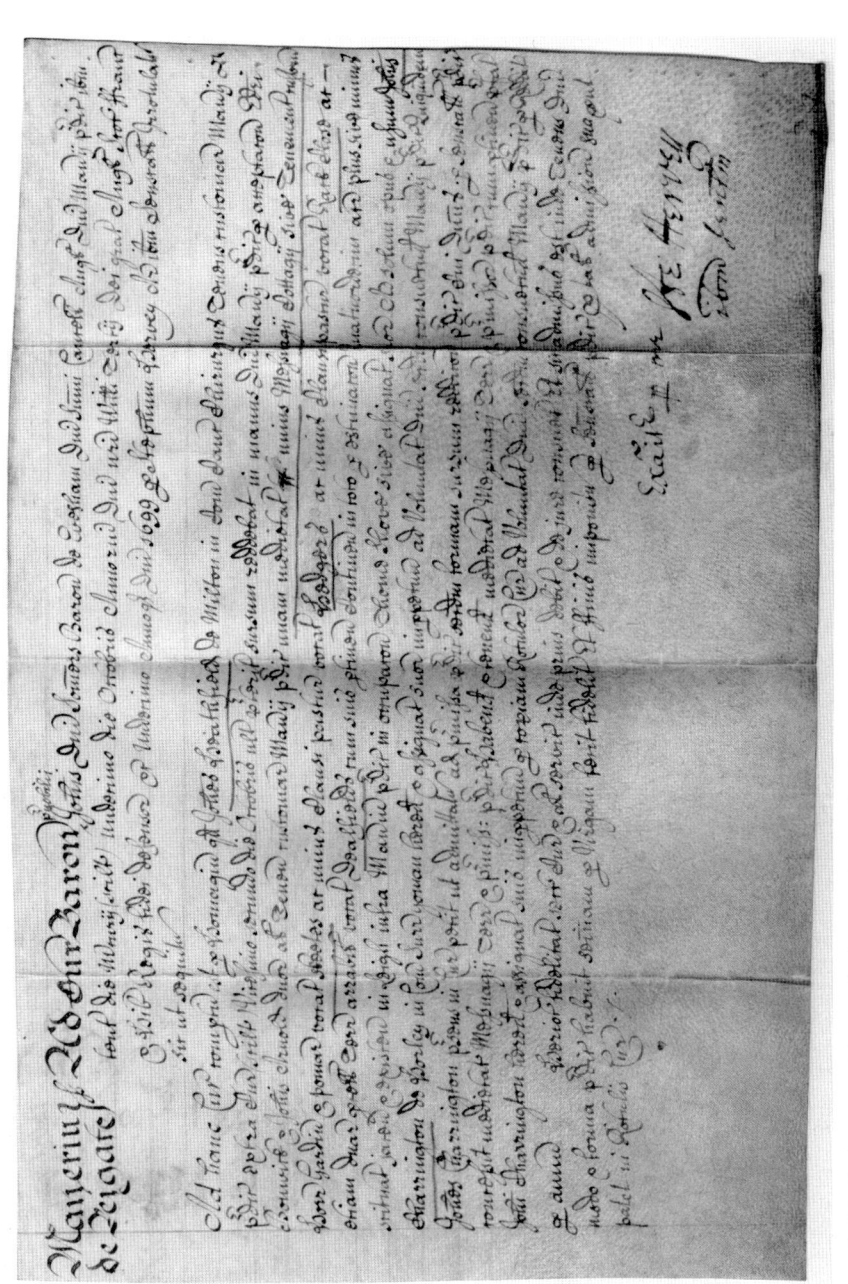

Copyhold Admittance, with recital of Surrender, of a half part of a messuage, barn, orchard and land in Leigh, Surrey, 11 October 1699. John Heathfield (line 5) surrenders the property to the use of John Charrington (lines 10/11). From the Manuscripts and Special Collections of the University of Nottingham, reference Ne D 5296.

ad opus et usum ... de ... heredum et assignorum suorum imperpetuum secundum consuetudinem manerii predicti
to the use and benefit of ... of ..., his heirs and assigns for ever, according to the custom of the manor aforesaid.

Copyhold

Et ad eandem curiam venit prefatus ... et cepit de ... prefato domino per senescallum suum predictum terras predictas cum pertinentiis
And to the same court came the aforenamed ... and took from the aforenamed lord, through his aforesaid steward, the aforesaid lands, with the appurtenances,
habendum et tenendum prefato ...et heredibus suis secundum consuetudinem manerii predicti imperpetuum per redditus et servicia inde prius debita et de jure consueta
to have and to hold to the aforenamed ... and his heirs, according to the custom of the aforesaid manor, for ever, by the rent and services formerly due in respect thereof and by right accustomed,
et dat domino pro fine pro ingressu ...
and he gives to the lord as a fine for entrance ...
et admissus est inde tenens
and he is/was admitted as tenant thereof,
et fecit fidelitatem
and he made fealty.

A typical "three lives" copyhold is as follows;

Super quo domini per senescallum suum concesserunt predictum mesuagium cum pertinentiis Samueli Lucas Marie uxori eius et Elizabethe uxori Johannis Lucas senioris
Whereupon the lords, through their steward, granted the aforesaid messuage, with the appurtenances, to the aforesaid Samuel Lucas, Mary his wife, and Elizabeth the wife of John Lucas senior
habendum et tenendum eisdem Samueli Marie et Elizabethe pro termino vitarum earum et eorum alterius diutius viventis successive ad voluntatem dominorum secundum consuetudinem manerii predicti
to have and to hold to the same Samuel, Mary and Elizabeth, for the term of their lives, and of whichever of them [is] the longer living, successively, at the will of the lords, according to the custom of the aforesaid manor,
reddendum inde annuatim dominis et successoribus suis ad festa usualia ... et duos capones ac faciendum omnia alia onera servicia et consuetudines inde prius debita et de iure consueta ac herriettum cum acciderit
yielding annually in respect thereof, to the lords and their successors, at the usual feasts, ..., and two capons, and doing all other charges, services and customs formerly due and of right accustomed in respect thereof, and heriot when it shall have fallen due.
Et dant dominis de fine pro totali statu et ingressu sic in premissis habendo ...
And they give to the lords, as a fine, for thus having all their estate and entrance into the premises, ...
et predictus Samuel fecit dominis fidelitatem et admissus est inde tenens sed fidelitas predictarum Marie et Elizabethe respectuatur quousque etc
and the aforesaid Samuel made fealty to the lords, and was admitted as tenant thereof, but the fealty of the aforesaid Mary and Elizabeth is respited until etc.